You *Still* Talk Too Much

A Wife's Guide to **Stand** as a Silent Warrior

You
Still Talk
Too Much

A Wife's Guide to **Stand** as a Silent Warrior

Tanya Denise

This book is dedicated to my *behind-the-scenes* crew. They are the ones who labored with me, prayed with and for me, fasted with me, and poured into me and my marriage, through every test, trial, and triumph.
No matter what came, they encouraged me with the Word of God, held me accountable, comforted me, held my arms up, stood in the gap for me, got in the trenches with me, wiped away the tears, sweat, and blood, and stood with me. They too are Silent Warriors.

Contents

"Therefore, put on the full armor of God, so that when the day of evil comes, you may be able to **stand** your ground, and after you have done everything, to **stand**."

- *Ephesians 6:13 NIV*

Dear sis,

Do you want your marriage? No....seriously?! Do you *want* your marriage? If the answer is a resounding, heartfelt, "Yes," great! You are in the right place.

If there is uncertainty or doubt, continue reading because my prayer is that something within you (the warrior) will awaken and arise. If the answer is, "no," take a leap of faith and continue reading anyway. I believe you will learn something that will help you right where you are.

For this journey, I am going to need your undivided attention. I need you to get quiet so you can hear. I am going to share some hard truths, reality checks, real-life experiences, and biblical principles with you. I am not here to condemn you, criticize you, judge you, or beat you down. I am not here to persuade you to make any decision whatsoever.

I am not a licensed counselor or therapist. I am not an ordained minister. I am not a marriage or relationship expert. I am a married woman who has also been divorced. I have been broken, wounded, and restored in relationships and marriage. I have endured and overcome abandonment, abuse, addiction, and adultery, in marriage. I have healed in many areas and still have some healing to walk out in other areas.

I am a believer. I believe *in* God. I believe God. I believe that Jesus is my personal Lord and Savior. I believe in the Bible. I am here to share with you my journey and what I have learned. I am here to share what has and has not worked for me and other married women I know who have been doing this married thing for a long time.

No matter the state of your marriage in this moment, there is hope. How do I know? Because I had loss all hope in my marriage. I had given up. But God restored my hope, and He restored my marriage. More importantly, He restored my faith.

This book is for wives who want change and want God's will. It is for wives who pray or those who are at least willing to learn how to effectively pray. This book is for real wives. Not the reality show women who are married, but kingdom women who are serious about their Father's business.

Let me be clear...this book is for believers. It is for Christian women who are married and who believe in God and the Bible. It is not just for those who believe but for those who want to walk in truth and do marriage God's way. God established marriage, He designed it; why would you not want to do it His way?

When we do not do marriage God's way, we set ourselves and our marriage up for failure. We are not called or destined to fail. The Bible says to put on the full armor of God, so that when the day of evil comes, you may be able to **stand** your ground. We are called to **stand** and having done all else to **STAND** (Ephesians 6:13)!

This book is going to help you **stand** as a silent warrior and maintain your position. If you have not read *You Talk Too Much: A Wife's Guide to Becoming a Silent Warrior*, I encourage to you read that book when you get chance because you need the tools it shares for the *becoming* phase. You also need to under**stand** what you are getting into because once you make a decision to go to war in the spirit for your marriage and to take a **stand**, you are shaking things up and all hell is likely to break loose! Welcome to the process and journey on how to arise and **STAND** as a silent warrior!

Blessings, *Tanya*

CHAPTER 1

Ready or Not

Marriage is not for punks. No one told me what to expect within marriage the first or second time around. I thought I was ready for it. I thought I had prepared for marriage. I read books, prayed, watched sermons, attended workshops, and consulted married couples, long before getting married. I honestly thought I was ready.

I was single for several years between my first and current marriage. I took time to learn more about me. I took time to date and learn what I liked and did not like. I took time to heal from my divorce and my past relationships. I attended counseling, joined a church, and spent time alone for a season. Somewhere in all the time I took, it was not enough to prepare me for what was to come.

Or maybe it was, and I missed it. Maybe I was too busy taking time for me and not giving enough time to my relationship with God and understanding what that meant. Maybe I was too caught up in checklists and recommendations that I missed the bottom line. Nevertheless, I tried. I did what I knew to do. I did what I was encouraged and advised to do, by elders, the books I read, and the workshops I attended.

I thought I had it together. Not all the way. However, I was doing well. I had a decent job. I had decent credit. I had savings (no matter how small it was). I had my own car. I had my own place. I was raising my two sons on my own. I was an active member of my church. I managed my own business. I had a lot going on, and it was good stuff. Yes, life had thrown me several lemons and I made lemonade out of all of them. Still, nothing (in the natural) could have prepared me for what was to come.

It took a few years for it to sink in. My heart had to break, and my knees became bruised before I finally got it. I had to die...to self, completely. Are you willing to die for the sake of your marriage? Are you willing to die to your own will, ambition, and desires, in exchange for God's will and desire for you and your marriage? Are you willing to lay aside "everything that hinders and the sin that so easily entangles" (Hebrews 12:1)?

Marriage was designed by God with purpose and on purpose. The purpose of marriage is to mirror and illustrate the relationship between Christ and

His Bride (the believer). Marriage is not about happiness, rather it is about holiness. So many people marry for happiness and they enter the union with unrealistic expectations. When those expectations are unmet many will back out or give up.

Marriage is not for the faint of heart; again, marriage is not for punks. You must be willing to put in the work. You must be willing to fight for what is right and fight the right way. In marriage, you will learn more about yourself, your spouse, your faith, and God, than ever, IF you do it right.

Marriage is ministry. Period. No one told me, no one warned me, and perhaps you feel the same way. Marriage is not a game and it is not a fairy tale. In real life, it does not look like the movies and if your marriage looks like the movies you may not be doing it God's way and other things may be going on. That's a different book for a different time.

Marriage is a sacrifice. So many start the race, then tap out. They drop off or fall out before they finish. Most of them drop off or fall out just before the breakthrough. This was me.

I was a runner. I had a history of running. I learned to run from the first sign of relationship conflict. I became good at cutting off and moving on. In fact, I was proud of my ability to do so.

Except for one, every relationship I had been in with a boy or man I ended. This means I broke it off for one reason or another. I had never been dumped and I was proud about the track record. (The "except for one" instance was a unique situation. I wasn't dumped, yet I was abandoned, in a weird way. You can read more about this in my memoir *Menorpause*).

When I got married, the first time, at the first hint of conflict or trouble, I was ready to run. It was an automatic, built-in, defense I had developed. Somehow, I knew marriage was different and I tried to adapt. I managed to remain in my first marriage beyond the initial conflict for nearly five years before I ended up running without looking back.

By the time I married again, I really thought I had worked through my *stuff*. I walked through a season of singleness and celibacy. When I decided to date, I was very particular, and I held the reign of control. I entered a new level of womanhood this time around as I mastered some things about myself.

I sent my current husband through a few ringers before we committed to marriage. Once he passed the tests and we said, "I do," I figured all was well. I knew to not do what I did before in marriage. I was older, wiser, and this was a completely different person. When we faced challenges, I knew that running was not the answer and I knew to pray.

In my book, *You Talk Too Much: A Wife's Guide to Becoming a Silent Warrior*, I share my experience of learning to pray for my husband and my marriage. I also introduce the early phase of becoming a silent warrior. This is a term my mother-in-law used when she encouraged me to pray for my marriage and I adopted the title.

A warrior is a fighter. A warrior is someone who shows or has courage. A *silent* warrior is also a fighter, yet one who fights in the spirit. The Bible says that the weapons of our warfare are not carnal. If the weapons are not carnal, the war or battle is not carnal. It is spiritual, and we cannot fight a spiritual battle with carnal weapons.

A silent warrior knows the power of prayer. A silent warrior applies wisdom and intention to their words, knowing when to speak and when to be quiet. The Bible says, there is a time to be silent and there is a time to speak (Ecclesiastes 3:7). How does one learn the difference? Wisdom.

Becoming a silent warrior does not mean you never speak up, share your thoughts, ideas, or opinion. It does not mean that you lose your voice. It simply means that you apply wisdom and seek to remain in tune with Holy Spirit, so you know the when, what, and why. Wisdom will guide you in knowing when it is time to speak and when it is time to be silent. This applies to life, in general, but here we are applying it to marriage.

I went through the process of becoming a silent warrior. I watched God move in me, my husband, and our marriage. Somewhere amid it all I became too comfortable and I left my post. What does that mean? It means I did not maintain my position and **stand** my ground. The moment there was any loose footing, the enemy came in and he came in like a flood!

See, I accepted the position as a silent warrior and then tried to withdraw. I put on my armor, loaded up, fired, shot, was shot at, and retreated due to injury and inconsistency. I backed down. I loss faith.

That's not the way to win! We (believers) don't give up or back down! We are promised the victory, so why would we want to give up or back down? Yet, it happens. Life happens. Disappointment happens. We are human, in this world, but not of it, yet we are still in it. We are still in a flesh body, with emotions having to navigate the issues of life. If we are not careful, we can become more consumed with life than God, lose our footing, and fall.

The problem is we do more talking than praying. I am guilty. Even after releasing my first book about marriage and practicing the tips and tools shared, I failed. I did not talk *as much* to my friends about my marriage, but I still shared things that I was not supposed to share. I prayed one thing, then spoke against that very prayer by opening my mouth and updating a friend or telling her what had been going on. I prayed, but not enough. I stopped talking as much, but I still talked *too* much.

What are you saying about your marriage? What are you saying about your husband? Who are you saying it to? All this matters.

The Bible says we are snared by the words of our mouth (Proverbs 6:2). Snared means *trapped*. Do you under**stand** that you can desire one thing and trap yourself into another with your mouth? I had to eat some of my words and let me tell you it hurt like hell! My marriage almost failed because of my mouth.

Is your marriage suffering because of your mouth? Are you trapped by your own words as it relates to your marriage? Is your union failing because you always need to vent or get something off your chest? Are you talking about your husband to others? Shut up and pray!!

As wives, the greatest power and influence we have is prayer. It is a resource and a weapon. It is how we gain wisdom, knowledge, instruction, and guidance on how to navigate life and marriage! Our lives and our marriages can either thrive or fail based on our prayer life and what we speak!

CHAPTER 2

The End of the Beginning

My marriage was over. I thought there was no turning back. We had faced so many challenges and difficulties. We had hurt one another so much I thought the only way for any resolve and healing was to divorce.

Although we started off saying divorce was never an option, it was always an option. It is always a choice. No matter how spiritual you think you are, when the going gets tough you'd be surprised how many options become a reality.

My husband and I are believers. We believe in God, the Bible, and we have both accepted Jesus as our personal Lord and Savior. We prayed on our first date and we fasted before he proposed marriage.

In the beginning of our relationship, we started off praying together, regularly. We read the Bible together, we read, discussed, and worked through devotions, and we watched Marriage Today with Jimmy and Karen Evans.

We joined and attended church. We went to marriage retreats, conferences, and had regular date nights, and regular sex. Yet, our marriage reached a point that seemed to have no return.

We were not perfect. Please under**stand** that. We did not do everything right, yet we did our best and we aimed to keep God front and center, initially. The moment we stopped allowing God the authoritative position and leadership role in our marriage, all hell broke loose.

Every conversation turned into an argument. In fact, there were not many conversations. A simple *good morning* would go left and turn into yelling, raising our voices over one another, walking away, or hanging up the telephone.

Things got ugly. Very. Things got violent, too, on both sides. I broke stuff, threw stuff, as a response, and told my husband to go be with someone else. He had his share of inappropriate behavior, too, but this is about me. Let's just say there was all sorts of ungodly things going on.

The noise from our pain was loud. It was deafening. I could not hear him. He could not hear me. *We* could not hear God.

I was certain we were headed for six feet under. In fact, the marriage was three feet under, with a strong stench of death. Divorce papers had

22

been filed for the third time and we were separated. We were not legally separated, yet we were living apart and barely talking.

It was clear. It was evident. It was over.

***

IN THE BEGINNING

My husband, Rafael, and I met in Florida. I shared the following story in my book, *You Talk Too Much: A Wife's Guide to Becoming a Silent Warrior*. In case you have not read that book (yet), I am sharing this story again. If you have read that book, consider this a refresher with purpose (and more details).

I was training in Florida for a new job back in California, which is where I was born and raised. My new job required out-of-state training and originally planned to send me to Michigan. One morning, my manager called me into his office and asked me if I would prefer to go to Florida instead. I had never been to Michigan or Florida so it did not matter to me. My manager gave me until the next day to make a decision.

I went home that night and I shared the information with my mother, my best girlfriends Trina and Kisha, and the guy I was seeing at the time. They all recommended that I choose Florida for training. Fate was in action.

The following morning, I went to my manager and gave him the news.

He smiled and said, "I think you will be happy with your choice to go to West Palm Beach, Florida."

After leaving his office and returning to my desk, I immediately hopped on the computer and I Googled *West Palm Beach*. The pictures I saw were stunning. The beaches, the palm trees, the excitement began to brew. I was was going to Florida for the first time and I was elated.

I left California on Sunday, April 24th. I had no idea that it was Rafael's birthday because we had not met, yet. I had a connecting flight from the Los Angeles International airport (LAX) to Dallas Fort Worth International airport (DFW). From Dallas, I arrived to West Palm Beach late afternoon.

The sun was bright, the air was warm, I had a company paid rental car, and prepaid reservations at an extended stay four-star hotel. I drove from the car rental hub of the Palm Beach International (PBI) airport, to my hotel in the heart of the city. I pulled up to the hotel in awe. It was beautiful. It was regal and it was my home for the next few months.

My hotel suite was prepaid for my entire stay. When I arrived to the hotel, guest relations said they were expecting and waiting for me. This may have been **stand**ard customer service but I felt like royalty, especially when I walked into my hotel room and my name was on the telephone and television screens.

I had a full kitchen, bedroom, and living area. The bathroom was luxurious with an amazing walk-in shower. When I walked to the window I was grateful. I had a beautiful view of Palm Beach island. This was an experience for the books and one that will always be cherished.

I was excited about my new job, meeting new people, making friends, and exploring my temporary home. My girlfriend, Myrna, encouraged me to create a profile on a dating site while I was there. I thought her idea was crazy. I was in a new town, a new state, and although excited, I was nervous. Meeting a man was the furthest thing from my mind.

Besides, I was dating someone back in California. The relationship was more of a situationship. We had been dating for a year and a half. It was moving slowly with no direction or goal. I cared about the guy but I believe we were both still there, in the situation, due to comfort and not purpose.

Myrna's idea to date while in a new state made me nervous. I had an interest and hobby of watching shows like *Snapped, the First 48*, and *Who the Bleep Did I Marry*, on the Investigate Discovery channel. I had watched way too many episodes of dates gone wrong and I didn't want to be on any of the shows. I thought if I joined a dating site in this new state, I'd be a victom on an episode of one of my favorite shows, for sure.

My new job was great. I clicked well with the ladies at the office right off the bat. I am a personable person so that was to be expected. I even managed to plan a girls night with the ladies at the office to get away from work and out of my hotel room. They were not as excited to get together and go out often because West Palm Beach was home for them. I was a tourist and wanted to explore.

After a month of being in Florida, my routine became mundane. I would get up, shower, throw on comfy clothes, go have breakfast in the dining area of the hotel, go back to my hotel room to get dressed, and drive to work. After training all day with my superstar trainer, Jena, I would get off, stop by one of the local restaurants or the grocery store, pick up dinner and head to the hotel. Some days I went to the gym and other days I went to the beach, which was very close by. All that became old, fast.

I had spoken with the guy I was dating a few times while being in Florida. I missed him because I was used to him but I really missed companionship. After a few dry phonecalls with him and a few bored nights in my hotel room, I finally decided to take Myrna's suggestion and I created a dating profile.

"IT'S A MATCH"

Tinder. Easy peasy, right?! Swipe, swipe, swipe… swipe my life away! Sigh! I had a few instant matches and so the game began.

Swipe, swipe, swipe, swipe, swipe. I knew this was not going to last long. I was bored and uninterested on the first night. I was never one to initiate conversation because I preferred the man to do that. Once I had a few matches, I found myself engaged in online conversations very quickly. Some were dry and boring. Some were entertaining and funny. Some were blocked sooner than I could log out.

I was not looking for a relationship, a hookup, or anything of that nature. I most certainly was not looking for a lifetime partner. I made that clear on my profile.

One evening as I was swiping, I came across a photo of a very handsome man. Seeing his photo stopped me in my tracks, or my swipes. He was not my typical *type* but it didn't matter because I was not looking for a relationship or a hookup. He was a pretty boy, by my definition. He was brown skinned, a bit on the lighter side, and he had black, thick, wavy hair, and thick, wavy eyebrows. He had full, smooth lips, a light beard, and he was fine fine. His name was Rafael.

His profile indicated that his birthday was around the same time as mine. He was an artist, a writer, liked to cook, and he could spell. The fact that he could spell was attractive. You wouldn't believe some of the messages guys would send to me without spell check or spell sense.

This guy was different. He seemed interesting and I liked the fact that he had information on his profile and several pictures. I swiped right and it was an instant match (which means he had already swiped right on my profile).

It took a couple of days before he reached out to me, but when he did he was a gentleman. After messaging back and forth for several days, we exchanged telephone numbers. Our communication continued for several days using text messaging. Then, we finally had our first telephone conversation.

We talked for a couple of hours. This was right up my alley. He happened to be a good listener and he was quite engaging. He was a communicator, like me, and he held great conversation. We did not have any awkward silences or long pauses. We talked as if we had known one another forever. He was not looking for a relationship, a hookup, or anything of that nature either and he understood my visiting circumstances. It was a jackpot!

After a few phonecalls, we decided to meet in person. He was going to be my new friend and give me a tour of Florida. We both enjoy the ocean so our first meeting and date was at the beach. After the face to face introduction, we enjoyed the warm sun, the gentle breeze, and the beautiful blue water, with our feet in the sand.

We talked and talked, for hours. We met at 5 p.m. on a Friday and we talked until 7 a.m. Saturday morning. Yes, we talked for 14 hours! I am not exaggerating! There was no hanky panky, we did not kiss, and we remained in public the entire time. We sat on the beach until sunset. Then, we went to the pier and sat out all night talking about almost everything. The conversation was so good neither of us wanted it to end and we honestly lost track of time.

We were so intrigued by one another, both wanting to under**stand** God's purpose for our meeting. He knew about the guy I was seeing back in California and I knew about the relationship he had recently gotten out of. We literally talked about any and everything, freely, and naturally. He was completely transparent and I needed that.

At one point, he was in the rental car with me in the passenger seat. He had to get out of the car for a moment. When he did, he left his cell phone. For me, that was new. I was so used to guys holding on to their phones for dear life and seeming so protective and secretive. Not this guy.

When we decided that I would drive to the pier (one of my safety measures was to not get in the car with him), as I was driving, his cell phone rang.

He answered and put the call on speaker. It was a woman. It was his ex wife and daughter's mother.

I heard the entire conversation as he briefly discussed seeing his daughter that weekend. Hearing their conversation said a lot to me because once again I was used to guys who kept things hidden or private but in a way that indicated dishonesty. Not this guy. He was an open book and I loved that about him.

While sitting at the pier after talking for hours, Rafael asked me if we could pray together. I think that is the moment I fell in love, if that's possible! I agreed to pray with him. We both took turns praying and it was a special experience.

THE PROGRESSION

After an amazing week with Rafael, I flew back to California to spend time with my children for the weekend before returning to work. Leaving Florida for just a few days seemed like the hardest thing to do. I was excited to see my children; however, I did not want to leave Rafael. It felt like I was leaving a part of me behind. It was the worst and best feeling I had experienced. We had a strong connection and a bond was quickly established.

When I arrived to California, the first thing I did was end the relationship with the guy I had been dating. I had met someone new and he had given me a new hope. I was not hoping for a relationship but even the establishment of the friendship with Rafael was such a breath of fresh air that I didn't want anything stale in my life. Besides I had learned more about Rafael in a week than I had known about the guy I was dating for a year and a half. It was eye opening.

I enjoyed a fabulous weekend with my children before going back to work in Florida. Again, it was a bittersweet feeling as I left my children, and was returning to work and to Rafael. We had planned to meet for dinner upon my return. I was going to pick up the rental car, go to my hotel, shower, and then change before meeting up with him.

When my plane landed in Florida, after texting my mother and children, I texted Rafael to let him know I had arrived. To my surprise, he was already at the airport waiting for me. This was the beginning of his sweet gestures and surprises for me.

Things were going really well. We spent every day together after our first meeting (except when I flew home to California, of course). We would see one another before work, text during the day, meet up for lunch, if we could, see one another after work, and we spent our off days together. We became inseparable and were very comfortable with one another. The reality however, was I lived in California and he lived in Florida.

We had several conversations about what we were supoosed to pursue or do with our meeting. Rafael initiated a fast and I agreed to it. We fasted for three days for clarity and direction concerning our meeting. He specifically sought God about proposing marriage and I sought God about his purpose in my life. At the end of the fast, I had peace about moving forward with a relationship.

I remember silently praying and asking God why this man had come into my life. He had so many qualities that I desired in a mate, but he was in Florida so it made no sense to me. I had no plans to relocate and no desire for a long distance relationship.

During my silent prayer, I asked God to give me a sign to confirm if Rafael was the man to love me. I prayed silently on purpose. I did not want the enemy to hear my prayer so that when my answer came I would know it was from God. I specifically asked God for a gesture. I needed God to prompt Rafael to do something that would move me, but only God knew it would move me.

The following day, during his lunch break, Rafael asked me to meet him in the parking lot of his apartment complex. I pulled up next to his work truck and he came over to open my door (like he always does). I turned to grab my purse, thinking I was getting out of the car, and when I turned back towards him, he had a bouquet of roses for me.

This may seem minor, to you; however, it was the exact gesture I prayed for. No one knew I prayed for this besides God. Rafael did not even know if I liked flowers because although we thought we talked about almost everything we did not talk about that. One reason I prayed for this gesture was because it was something that I desired, yet lacked in my previous relationships.

I began praying more about Rafael. I saw a lot of good qualities in him, things I said I wanted in a husband but I knew it had only been a short time since meeting. There was more to him, just like there was more to me. I asked God to show me what I was unable to see and needed to see because I did not want to make another mistake where relationships were concerned that would result in heartbreak.

One night, we were in the car at the gas station after Rafael had a hard day at work. After he pumped the gas and got back into the car, he started sharing things I had never heard him share before. He shared some of his fears, some of his struggles, and how he needed to grow more spiritually. I listened as he attempted to pour his heart out. Once again, God had heard and answered my prayer because he gave me a clear glimpse of what I had been unable to see and needed to know before moving forward with Rafael. Nothing he shared was alarming or shocking. In fact, I felt equipped to support him where he was and where he wanted to go.

A few days later, Rafael came by my hotel on his lunch break. It was the weekend and I was off from work but he was not. When I got into his work truck, which was parked just outside of my hotel, he kissed me on the cheek, then he handed me some cash. I asked him what it was for. He explained it was a tip he had received from work and he was just giving me some money to put in my pocket. I did not need the money but I appreciated his gesture and the gift. I thanked him, folded the money, and tucked it inside of my pocket.

His break was ending and I needed to return to my hotel room from his work truck.

As I was getting out of the truck he said, "What's your ring size?"

I stopped in my tracks. I turned to look at him and responded, "Seven."

He smiled and told me he would call me when he got off work.

THE PROPOSAL

I went back to my hotel room, nervously excited. I called my girlfriend, Toby, right away to tell her about Rafael's question about my ring size. She squeeled with enthusiasm and we laughed together. She and I had prayed during my fast with Rafael. Toby is an ordained minister and she was a close friend whom I trusted. She told me after we prayed that she believed Rafael was my husband. I never spoke that to him or anyone else.

As she and I were on the telephone, my excitement was robbed by fear. It had only been three weeks since I had met this man in person. I wondered if he was seriously planning to propose. I wondered if we were moving too fast. I wondered what I would say if he proposed.

Toby and I talked through my fears. She also prayed with and for me. I decided to trust God as I had been doing. Things seemed almost too good to be true, yet there was a steady, consistent flow, and peace.

On June 22nd, my mother's birthday, Rafael and I planned to meet for dinner after work. I was still in Florida working. We had previously visited several restaurants around the city already. He asked me where I wanted to go this night and although we had already been there, it was my favorite restrautant, so I chose Applebee's. He attemtped to suggest going somewhere else but I was insistent about going to my favorite place. Besides they were having karoake night and back in California the Applebee's I had been to never had karoake night.

We arrived to the restaurant and were seated. It was nearly empty. Somehow we had missed karoake night. We decided to still stay to eat and spend time together. It was late at night and we both had work the next day so I opted for a salad and he had a drink. As we were sitting and talking, he reached for my hand from across the table. I placed my hand into his and he began to express his heart.

My memory escapes me everything he said but it was something to the fact of loving me deeply in such a short time and believing God sent me as a birthday present to him (based on my arrival date to Florida). He expressed how he still had some things to work on and areas to grow in but needed his life partner to be by his side during the process. His said he believed I was her – his life partner. Then, he pulled out a ring and proposed. I did not hesitate to say, "Yes." In fact, he did not just ask me to marry him, he asked me to "take this journey" with him.

In hindsight, he was more clear than I thought because he presented himself with a disclaimer. Yet, the excitement of being proposed to in the height of a summer romance blinded me from absorbing and fully understanding what was wrapped into what he was saying to me. This is not a testament of regret, yet a reflection to being alert to truth when it is presented

Prior to the engagement, Rafael had taken me to meet his mother, one of his brothers, one of his sisters, his daughter, his ex-wife, and a few of his friends. His mother and I instantly connected. She even told me she had been praying for me. It was weird to hear, yet I understood she had been praying for a wife for her son and meeting me seemed to be the answer to her prayer.

Again, things were going really well. We talked a lot, laughed a lot, drove around town so that I could sightsee, we went out to eat, we had a lot of fun together, and we prayed together, regularly. We were now engaged with a promise to become husband and wife.

My time in Florida eventually came to an end. It was time for me to fly back home to California with no return date. Rafael and I decided we were going to try to maintain a long distance relationship and figure things out (with the engagement) over time. I would visit him and he would visit me, we would video chat, and talk over the telephone.

Looking back, we were crazy! We could have very well became an episode of one of my favorite crime investigation shows. We did not know one another as well as we thought, yet we were going about things like we had known one another for ages. It was good, it was easy, and we trusted God, yet looking back I think we were crazy!

THE BIG MOVE

Two months after I left Florida, Rafael was scheduled to fly to California to visit me and meet my family on Labor Day weekend. He had a rountrip ticket because the original plan was for him to return home to Florida. The day before his flight, Rafael resigned from his job as a Cable Technician, packed up, and decided to relocate to California.

Talk about crazy faith! He had never been to my home. He had no idea how I really lived my life. I had no idea how he lived his life aside from our summer romance. It was a risk, a huge risk. It was a leap of faith. At the time, it was flattering that he would leave his hometown to pursue a life with me. Again, looking back we were crazy!

Rafael arrived to California and it felt surreal. I leaped into his arms when he came out of the gate at the airport! We had not seen each other in two months and it felt like forever, but here he was, to stay!

He met my sons, my mother, and my sister, right away. Within the first few days of being in California, he also met my brother, my uncle, and my grandfather. He asked my grandfather and my mother for my hand in marriage. They gave him their blessing.

Within a week of being in California, Rafael had a job and we were planning a wedding. Our vision was a beach wedding. Remember, we both loved the beach and it is where we had our first date. We just did not know how to bring two families who were 2,611 miles apart, together, for such an occasion, without it costing too much for them and for us.

Within four months we decided to elope and tell everyone later. We honored our parents by telling them first, the morning after. Then, we told our children. Then, we told our closest friends. Once those closest to us were informed of the news, we changed our Facebook statuses.

The elopement was beautiful. It was short and sweet. We did not dress up; we wore matching colored casual clothes. We privately exchanged vows in a small chapel. He cried while saying his vows, which caused me to cry, too. We went to dinner afterwards, then cosummated our marriage at the hotel on the Las Vegas strip. It was simple. It was inexpensive. It was done.

CHAPTER 3

The Process

We had such a beautiful beginning. Even before he came to California we had talked about what living together might look like. We established agreements and boundaries. We had a plan for how we wanted things to go. The plan worked for a little while, then things started to change.

You'll have to read my book, *You Talk Too Much*, to learn more about some of the earlier challenges Rafael and I faced. Let's just say all the praying and reading the Bible together that we did early on, went out of the window when real life started to happen. Things became tough. Reality was before us and we had not fully prepared for how to manage it.

I thought I was a good catch overall and I thought I was a good wife, but it is not up to me to make that assessment. (Note: You may think you are a good wife, but what does God think and what does your husband think?) When I thought I was expressing my feelings, to him I was nagging, I was hurting him, and damaging the marriage. When I thought we had conquered things (issues we discovered or created), he was holding onto them as unresolved. When I thought we were happy, he was miserable inside, losing faith, hope, and trust. We would have disagreements and quickly move past them so I thought we were sailing along just fine.

Yet, the waves grew and the boat was rocked. The waves were brutal, evenutally causing the boat to capsize! Everything fell out and fell over. There was a mess, a distaster at sea. Without much notice, we were shipwrecked.

I admit, I was not praying or reading my Bible the way I had in the beginning. We were not doing it together or individually. So naturally we drifted apart, starting on the inside. A friend of mine, Tamora, says that if we are not intentionally connecting, we are unintentionally disconnecting. This is true and my husband and I were disconnecting.

I thought we were connecting on date nights. Date nights mattered to *me*. He thought we were connecting during sex. Sex mattered to *him*. We were communicating, but not effectively. We were learning and growing, yet growing apart in that we did not know how to address some of things we were facing. I am talking about day to day, common things. As adults, we had our way of doing things and even though we had made agreements and set boundaries, naturally people fall back into what is familiar and comfortable.

We both had unknowingly built a wall around our hearts and neither was letting the other inside. God was not first and foremost in our lives any longer. We had abandoned Him and tried to manage marriage on our own. Eventually, it all came crashing down.

I started praying, again. I started fasting, again. I had others pray and fast with me. I tried seeking wise counsel and I tried keeping things to myself. I tried talking with my husband and I tried not talking with him. We tried counseling and therapy. We saw a female therapist twice until things blew up in her her office. We saw our Pastor a good four times before we stopped going to him for counseling and stopped going to church altogether. Nothing was working it seemed. Now, here we were: separated, living apart, and not talking, yet still married.

In my heart, I still loved my husband. I just didnt know how to show him. I didn't know how to fix what was broken. Neither did he. We had tried everything we knew, including accountability partners. None of it worked. We had tried everything humanly possible.

BUT GOD

Since nothing was working and we were not talking, my focus became my process of getting out of the marriage. My husband tried to call, text, and even stop by. I had changed the locks, I would ignore his calls, and I did not respond to his text messages. I had already filed for divorce, we were no longer living together, and I saw no point in communicating.

I must add that initially when we talked about separation it was intended to be a short break so we could heal and seek therapy. Our home was no longer peaceful, so a break seemed necessary to allow peace to be restored. My vision was for him to rent a room somewhere, we'd attend therapy, go on dates, and work on our relationship with God and each other with a bit of distance. His vision was getting his own place instead of renting a room and deep within he felt like if we separated there was no reconciling down the road. The problem was we did not thoroughly discuss our visions or a plan for separation.

In hindsight and in case you are considering separation, in my opinion, it is not a good idea. Sometimes it is necessary. If abuse, addiction, and other serious things are going on, separation **with Godly counsel** should be considered. Key point: **with Godly counsel**. You need a plan with a goal and accountability. Otherwise the enemy is waiting for this gap to occur so he can slide in.

When the enemy slides in, he creates further distance and division between two people who are supposed to be the closest two people in the world – husband and wife. You go from sleeping together every night to sleeping alone many nights. You go from managing a home together, even with disagreements mixed in, to managing a place on your own. Everything changes when marital separation takes place. When done right and with Godly counsel, it can be great for the marriage. When not done right and without a plan, it can be disastrous.

I knew I needed support in the season I was in. I needed my close friends near me, not physically but just available for phone calls, prayer, and mid-day getaways. I knew that being alone could lead to depression and God only knows what else. So, I surrounded myself with support. Only a handful of friends who were praying women knew the state of my marriage. They prayed with and for me. They checked in on me. They made themselves available at a moment's notice and there were some late night, midnight, and early morning phonecalls. Many times I was unable to pray for myself so my friends prayed. They were not praying for the end of my marriage, however. They were praying God's will to be done in my life. For me, that meant to divorce.

I started praying and reading my Bible, again, regularly. Prior to this, I had reached a place where I stopped fighting in the spirit. I started fighting in the natural and it wore me out. When your battle is not against flesh and blood, and you fight in the flesh, you will lose every time and it will drain you.

I had a weekly prayer call with three girlfriends. I had a weekly prayer meeting with Christian business women. I was in several online wife support groups. I listened to sermons every morning and evening. I had to surround myself with the right type of support and that was God's Word and those who sought His way and His will.

In addition to getting myself back on track spiritually, I set up a structured routine for work, business, and dove in. I created new goals and a new plan for my home, my finances, my business, started a second business, and eventually a third. I set daily goals and slayed them one by one.

I felt empowered and strong. I appeared empowered and strong to others who knew nothing about the state of my marriage. On the outside, things looked normal. Deep within, I was hurting.

One evening while working on a project for my business, I received a notification from Facebook Messenger. It was my friend Tamora. At that time she was just a woman I had recently met and befriended.

Tamora sent a few voice recordings. The first recording was her asking me how I was doing. She said she noticed that I tend to reach out to her and others to check on them but this time she was checking on me. Then, she started ministering to me in the recordings.

She spoke about my situation not even knowing it. I knew it was God who had given her the insight she had. We had no mutual friends who knew my situation. After she was done speaking, she prayed for me, in the recordings. Her words and prayer penetrated my heart. The walls came crashing down, so did the tears.

I was hurting and I thought I was healing. By choosing to focus on my spiritual growth during the separation, I had finally re-positioned myself to a posture where God could do the work needed. I was focused on becoming a better version of myself and not beating myself up for what I thought was another failed marriage. Yes, another. I had been married and divorced before so that reality would attempt to slap me in the face and make me feel unworthy. Yet, I knew better and had to focus on what I knew.

I was finally not blaming my husband or myself for the state of the marriage. I had released it all to God. I had forgiven my husband and I had asked for forgiveness for my part in it all and was ready to trust God with my new life.

Tamora allowed God to use her to show me myself. Her messages penetrated the walls I had built around my heart in effort to self protect. Once penetrated, those walls could no longer **stand** in the presence of the Almighty God. They came crashing down! Through her I realized that I was not healing, I was coping. I was covering my pain with work and God wanted to do some work in me.

I am naturally an overachiever and my coping method for many years has been to accomplish things. I have a tendency to bury myself in work, set goals and focus on tackling them. I am task oriented so it feels good when I tackle my list and slay my goals.

On the flip side, I have the ability to drown out anything going on around me through burying myself with work. I can become laser focused on the task or the goal and tune out any pain or threat of it. Again, this is coping, not healing and I had done this not only in the past but in my marriage. This time God wanted more for me. He did not want me to cope. He wanted me to heal and grow.

THE REBIRTH OF THE SILENT WARRIOR

One day, not long after I received the message from Tamora, while in prayer I heard God say, "*Pursue your husband, pursue your marriage, like I pursue you, with love.*" My eyes were closed, but I opened them. I was actually on a group prayer call at the time and when I opened my eyes, the host said, "I hear God saying *pursue.*" Talk about instant confirmation!

I thought I was losing it, yet I knew what I heard and I knew it was God. It had been a little while since I could hear from God so clearly. I grabbed my pen and I wrote in my journal what I heard. With tears welled up in my eyes to the point I was unable to see, I said aloud, "I don't even know why I still love this man!" Then, I heard, "*You love him because I AM LOVE and I AM in you.*" Tears burst from my eyes and down my cheeks. Before I knew it I was bawling like a baby!

I began praying in the spirit. God's voice was clear but my feelings weren't. I had mixed emotions. I was hurt. I was broken. I was wounded. I wanted my marriage but I had come to believe I had married the wrong man. I felt like we had reached a point of no return. We had said and done so many mean and hurtful things to one another and I was willing to chalk it all up as a lesson and move on. Afterall, we finally had peace. He was in his own place and I was in the place I fought very hard to remain in. There were no more arguments because at this point we were not even talking.

I whispered to God, "Lord, if this is from you, you are going to have to confirm and prove it." He said, *"I know what has been done and I will take care of it all. Will you trust me?"*

God continued speaking to me that morning. What He told me was profound and clear. I was awakened and ready to do what God said, yet I did not feel equipped. It made no sense in the natural. I hadn't talked with my husband in nearly three weeks. We did not even talk for his birthday or mine. In fact, I had purposely avoided his calls and I had ignored his text messages. I was preparing myself mentally for divorce.

The final word that day that caused me to answer the call and obey without a doubt was when God asked, *"Will you trust me?"* I cried. How was I going to tell God no? Did I trust God despite the state of my marriage? Did I trust God with my wounded heart? Did I trust God with the man I married? I had finally gotten quiet enough to hear from God and THIS is what He was telling me?!

God began to remind me of the beginning days – the story I just shared with you. He reminded me of *when* I arrived to Florida (on Rafael's birthday), how Rafael and I met, the gesture I prayed for, the revelations I prayed for, and how He had answered my prayers one by one. God reminded me of the small, yet clear confirmations that I had up to the point of separation.

Then, God reminded me of one particular huge blowout within the marriage where I just knew it was over for good. Yet after praying, during that occasion, God said, "My will is ressurrection, restoration, and reconcilliation." God said He would *ressurect* my marriage, *restore* the love, and *reconcile* my husband and I.

I thought I was going crazy. I had filed the divorce papers (for the third time). Everything pointed to the end of this union. I was certain my husband hated me by now and had probably moved on with someone else. Yet, I heard from God and I knew in my heart I had to trust God.

I wanted to trust God and do His will. I asked, "What next?" and I was prompted to go on a three-day water fast. Three days, no solid food, no social media, and set times to pray.

This fast was not like any other fast I had gone on. It was not difficult to deny my flesh as it had been in the past with other fasts. I had energy and felt strengthened. I made sure to pray and spend time seeking and hearing from God. I made sure to not let others know my plight, to limit my conversations, and to really focus.

During my prayer time, while on the fast, God began speaking to me more. At one point, as I lay on my bedroom floor praying in the spirit, I heard chains breaking. I don't know what broke and off of whom, me or my husband, but I know something broke.

God began giving me specific instructions daily on my new pursuit. The instruction included everything from calling my husband at specific times, texting specific words to him, preparing & delivering specific meals to him (not the withcraft way I was not a fan of cooking, yet my husband liked my cooking, so God had me cook meals he liked and deliver them to him). I was led to show up where I knew he would be, I was led to engage in sex with him, and much more. Each instruction was specific and rooted in love. I had to pray, before, during, and after each instruction. As I obeyed, my marriage transformed and so did my husband.

CHAPTER 4

Bootcamp

When my journey as a silent warrior began, it was working initially. I would pray and God would move. I could see and feel God's presence in my home and in my marriage. I could see God working on me and my husband. Then, there came a point where the more I prayed, things seemed to get worse. I thought this meant I was doing something wrong or things just weren't meant to be. I tried harder for a little while, and the more I tried, the worse things seemed to get. Eventually, I stopped praying as much just to get some relief from the attacks and battles.

Why am I sharing this? Bear with me. I have to paint a clear picture of my own journey, in order to assist you with your journey. I need you to see, know, and under**stand** that I am not perfect, and neither is my marriage. I need you to see, know, and under**stand** that I am a woman of faith, who has endured and overcome addiction, abandonment, abuse, and adultery, in marriage. Yet, I am still here, as in I am still **stand**ing for my marriage, and God has been good.

As I reflect on my process of becoming a silent warrior, I have to admit the truth. The truth is I was praying, but I was pity-pat or patty-cake praying. What does that mean? I had cute prayers. I had perfectly, typed prayers that I poetically read. I was pity-patting and patty-cake praying when a war for my marriage was going on.

I became a warrior in distress. Pity-pat praying and patty-cake praying will wear you out. You will exert energy with no reward. You will aim and miss. You will waste time thinking you are doing something yet will see no result because it's not as serious as you say it is.

Imagine having a gun in hand and just firing bullets, left and right. You're just shooting, and your accuracy is all off. See, I joined the battle but did not stay to fight. I thought one lil ole prayer was gonna cut it. Do not get me wrong. Prayer is prayer. You don't need some long, drawn-out laundry list to read or pray to be effective. Prayer is communication with God and it's a two-way street. You talk with God and God talks with you.

I was praying as a weakling. I was praying as someone who did not know or under**stand** their authority. I was crying out to God. *He hurt me. Do you see what he did God? Why is this happening? I don't deserve this.* Woe is me.

Are your prayers saturated with woe is me? Are you praying as a weakling, as someone who does not know or under**stand** your power and authority? Are you praying about the wrong things?

The Bible says, "You have not because you ask not and when you ask you ask amiss (James 4:2-3)." This means you ask for the wrong reasons and with the wrong intent. Is your heart right when you go to God concerning your husband and your marriage? Are you pity-pat and patty-cake praying like I was?

I was not praying with authority. I was not praying *and* **stand**ing firmly on the Word of God. I would ask God for one thing and if something happened that did not line up with what I had prayed, the prayer went out the window! I voided my own prayer when my actions and words did not match. We have to be careful and intentional with our words. Words have power! Your words can redirect your direction to the point you can be doing one thing, say another, and what you are doing will change to align with what you said.

Did you follow that? Let me give me an example. I would get upset with my husband and in my hurt state I would speak out of my mouth telling him to just go find someone else and move on. That is not what I wanted. Yet that is what I spoke because I was hurt. What I really wanted was for him to stop hurting me and to under**stand** me, but that is not what I said. I told my husband on multiple occasions to "just find someone else" and guess what? He did and when the mess hit the fan it hurt like hell.

The issue was I had not yet died to my flesh. This is the case for many of us when we are asking God for something, believing, and not seeing results. The Word works and God's Word cannot come back to Him void. When it comes to prayer, the true heart of the matter is our intent behind the prayer. Are we praying selfishly or soulishly? Are you praying God changes your husband or are you praying God change you? Are you praying for selfish gain or for kingdom purpose?

Many times, we are praying selfishly. We want our husbands to change so they can be better husbands for our benefit. We want to be heard, we want to do what we want to do, we want to be happy. Marriage is not about happiness. Marriage is about holiness. Happiness is a byproduct that we receive in marriage, but the purpose is holiness, kingdom business, and God's glory.

As I shared in my first book about marriage, I had worked on my mouth, but my mouth was still slick! I still had a lot to say and learning to pause and pray (Chapter 2 in *You Talk Too Much: A Wife's Guide to Becoming a Silent Warrior*) was a challenge. I can admit that after being hurt one too many times, it became extremely hard to be quiet. I am sure you can relate. I had my own ideas, feelings, thoughts, and opinions, and it seemed unfair to not be able to express them, so I was going to express them, and I did.

The problem was my husband was not under**stand**ing what I was expressing. I could repeat myself and he still did not seem to hear me or under**stand** me. I thought if I changed my words around regarding certain topics or points, that it would work. Well, it didn't.

Please under**stand** that often we are on a different level than our husbands. You may have wisdom in an area that he lacks wisdom in and vice versa. You may under**stand** a thing, a concept, or what have you better than he does. However, we cannot force someone to under**stand** something on a level they are not on. This is where prayer comes in to save the day. You can pray that God give your husband under**stand**ing and He will. He may not do it when you want Him to, and you have to accept that. The point is we cannot nag about a certain topic or force someone else to under**stand** or hear us. This can be very frustrating when that thing or topic is affecting your marriage.

It became awfully hard to trust that God would fight for me if I only stood on His word and held my peace. As time passed, I could literally hear

God tell me to hold my peace or to not say anything. I could hear, *"Be quiet,"* or *"Be still."*

I did it all for a little while. There were times when I failed to be obedient, however. I began to feel like I had to defend myself. I felt like I had to speak up for myself. Sometimes we should speak up, but God is our vindicator and most of the time God wants us to just be still and trust Him.

When Jesus was falsely accused, He did not say a word. He held His peace. He did not defend himself or try to argue his point. He knew the will of the Father and He trusted that.

Do you under**stand** the will of the Father for your marriage? Do under**stand** that to reign with Jesus, we must suffer with Him? What does this mean?

We live in a world where we think and believe that it is supposed to be about us. There are memes that suggest if it doesn't make me happy, then I don't want it in my life. This is a carnal or worldly viewpoint. I am not super holy or super religious and I am not trying to pressure you into being or feeling trapped in an unhappy marriage. But walk with me for a moment...

Jesus suffered. In His suffering He bore our sins. He died on the cross after being ridiculed, mistreated, falsely accused, lied on, and beaten. He is our Lord and Savior and He suffered. Do you really think you and I are not supposed to suffer or endure in this life? Especially in marriage.

The Bible says in marriage there will be trouble (1 Corinthians 7:28). Marriage was created to mirror the relationship between Christ and His bride – Jesus and the believer. Christ Jesus died for His bride, for the believer. Are you willing to die to self for your husband?

Yes, I know the Bible says that the husband is to love his wife as Christ loves the church (Ephesians 5:25). However, the Bible also says a believer is to deny himself and take up his cross and follow Jesus (Matthew 16:24). There is a laying down of one's own life and selfish ambition involved for both the husband and the wife.

I am not encouraging you to lay down and be a doormat. That is not what the Word says. I am encouraging you to surrender to God's Word about marriage and your life so that you can see God's Word at work in your marriage and in your life. Does that make sense?

Becoming a silent warrior is not just deciding to pray for your marriage. It is a decision to take a position. The position comes with responsibility. The responsibility comes with a pre-meditated attack by the enemy. To defeat the enemy, there is a process to go through and a training to undergo.

I did not know about the process until I was in it and came out of it. There are moments when I feel like I am still in it. I had to be stretched. My faith had to grow. I had to become fortified in my belief in

God's Word. I had to face myself and deal with my own stuff and stop looking to and at my husband. In the end, total surrender to God's will and God's way was required for me to see the truth.

You must under**stand** that deciding to **stand** for your marriage is a declaration of war. Satan has a mission to destroy families. He will do whatever it takes to tear apart as many marriages as possible. He wants to convince you why you should give up on your marriage and your husband. He wants to make you think that you married the wrong man.

CHAPTER 5

Help! I Married the Wrong Man

I messed up and I was sure of it. In my opinion, there were too many things wrong with my husband and my marriage for any of this to be God ordained. This became my thought pattern once trouble came into my marriage. I thought I was supposed to be happy. I thought life was supposed to get better once I was married. When I was unhappy and life did not get better, I was convinced I had married the wrong man.

For months I searched for confirmation that I had married the wrong man. I looked for sermons, teachings, scripture, and books. I needed direction and the steps to take to get out of my marriage, to fix the mistake I had made, and still be pleasing to God.

For a season, I was bound by the scripture that says God hates divorce (Malachi 2:16). I did not want to disappoint God or do anything that He hated. I had a counselor and therapist tell me I had married the wrong man and I should divorce him. I had ministers of the Gospel (Pastors, teachers, and leaders in the faith) tell me I had to stay married. Two vastly different perspectives that left me confused. So, I suffered in my marriage, unhappy and uncertain, beating myself up and meditating on how to get out.

Then, God began to show me some things. In the Bible, in the book of Genesis 29, we learn about Jacob, Rachel, and Leah. Jacob, the son of Isaac and grandson of Abraham, fled to his mother's brother, Laban. At the time, Jacob feared his twin brother, Esau, would kill him and that is why he fled. His uncle Laban allowed Jacob to stay with him.

Jacob saw and was captivated by the physical beauty of Rachel, Laban's daughter. He fell in love with Rachel and he desired to marry her. Laban thought it wise to give his daughter to Jacob than any other man and made him a deal. Jacob agreed to work seven years to get Rachel. He labored for the woman who was the apple of his eye. He did his part of the agreement and his uncle was supposed to do his part by allowing Jacob to have the woman who he believed was right for him.

Once Jacob had worked and put in the time he committed to, he went to Laban to claim his wife (Genesis 29:21). There was a feast and celebration for the marriage (the wedding). When the evening came, however, Laban sent Leah, his other daughter, to Jacob's quarters or bedroom. Jacob unknowingly made love to Leah, thinking it was his new bride Rachel. It must have been dark in the bedroom, right? When Jacob woke up the next morning and realized it was Leah in his bed, he panicked!! Jacob had been deceived. He had married the wrong one!! He had also just consummated the marriage.

Have you ever awakened and thought that you had married the wrong man? Imagine being in Jacob's shoes. There was no question about it. He married the wrong one – in his eyes!

I encourage you to study this text yourself, but ultimately Jacob was given Rachel, the *right* one and the one he wanted, after another seven years of hard work but this illustration of marrying the wrong one is important. The Bible shares that God showed favor to Leah, who to Jacob was the wrong one. Leah was unloved by her husband, he never wanted her to begin with. Leah had weary eyes and was no match to Rachel. Read it for yourself. The Bible describes Rachel as being physically attractive and Jacob desired and loved her. He loved Rachel so much that he worked 14 years to make her his wife.

Leah was Jacob's wife for seven years prior to sharing her husband with her sister (that is another book, prayer, and discussion). The point is, to Jacob he married the wrong one, yet he was blessed by the woman he thought was the wrong one. His destiny and purpose was tied to who he thought was the wrong one. Are you following?

Jacob thought Rachel was the one. That was who he worked to get, have, and be with, but who was presented to him and who he married was the right one for his destiny. The Bible illustrated that they became a wealthy family. It says that God pursued Leah and loved on her despite her being unloved by her husband. Check that out! God knew Leah's husband did not even love her, yet he blessed this woman and her marriage! Rachel, who Jacob thought was the one, was unable to conceive. She could not carry a seed or give birth. Glory to God!! But through Leah was conceived and birthed Ruben, Simeon, Levi, Judah, and more. Eventually through this family bloodline was birthed our Savior, Jesus Christ! Leah birthed purpose in Jacob's life and the world.

You may be thinking your husband is the wrong one and perhaps you could have married someone more compatible. However, God honors covenant!! Covenant is sacred. It is a spiritual contractual agreement. That agreement is not to be taken lightly and it is not just between you and your husband. God is a part of the covenant, too.

My point for referencing this text is Jacob and Leah were in covenant. God honored the covenant. Even though Jacob knew he married the wrong one, the covenant was blessed.

You are in covenant with your husband. Yes, you can choose divorce, but you do not have to. Again, the covenant is between you, your husband, *and* God. Even if you believe that you married the wrong man, God can still transform and bless your marriage. In fact, you may not have married the wrong man after all. Stay with me and hear me out.

There are more than 7.53 billion people on earth. Not everyone will choose marriage. If not, everyone chooses marriage that means not everyone has a chosen or designated spouse or soul mate because they have a choice to join themselves with someone or not. If those who choose to not get married remain single, then their spouse or said soul mate must choose someone else and this alone dispels the idea of having one soul mate.

I believe that we can be more compatible with certain people than others. I believe that we can have a stronger connection with certain people than others. God made Eve for Adam and she was his suitable helper. *Suitable* means acceptable, satisfactory, or fitting. She was acceptable for him. She was fitting for him. At that time, it was just her and him. Adam did not have a line up to choose from. He did not have options or choices.

With so many people in the world, now, there are options and choices. The range of suitability has expanded. You may be fitting or suitable for more than once person and you have to make a choice.

Granted, you may be best suited for one person, more than you are for someone else. So, it could be that your choice, your husband could have chosen a wife more suitable for him, but he chose you and you accepted becoming his wife. Now that you are in covenant and God honors covenant, God sees you as your husband's suitable companion and God can fix what you think is broken. He can make right what you think is wrong. He can bless your union the way He blessed Leah and Jacob.

This may be difficult to understand or accept, hence the reason for so many divorces. People accept that they have married the wrong person and they divorce. Some marry and divorce multiple times on a quest to find the "right one." As believers we have a charge to take God at His Word. You have the power to pray for true transformation in your husband and your marriage. In fact, being that you are in the covenant already, I believe you are anointed to pray your marriage through.

God's original plan for marriage was never divorce. Yes, the Bible specifically talks about divorce being permitted because of adultery and the hardness of hearts. But the action of divorce was permitted under the leadership of Moses and was still not God's original plan. Jesus said Moses permitted it. He did not say God permitted it.

No, this does not mean stay in any marriage, especially an abusive marriage. Note: If you are in an abusive relationship, which includes a serial cheater, or someone who is violently abusive, emotionally abusive, mentally, or financially abusive, I am not advocating that you stay. I am also not advocating that you end the marriage in divorce either. Only YOU know the circumstances and details of your marriage and only YOU can decide to stay married or not.

In cases of abuse, I believe separation is in order and the abusive and/or unfaithful spouse should get professional and spiritual help. The spouse who has been abused or cheated on should also get professional and spiritual help. Both spouses need to heal for the marriage to truly heal. For some couples, after healing comes reconciliation. For others, dissolution or divorce becomes the choice.

Notice the word *choice*. I hear couples say, "Divorce is not a choice!" Oh, but it is! It is always a choice, but it is not the only choice. No one can make the choice to leave or stay in a marriage besides the two people involved.

God gives grace to some people to endure and overcome exceedingly difficult and trying marriage journeys. Look at the book of Hosea in the Bible. Hosea was a prophet. Gomer was his wife. She was promiscuous. She was a harlot, a whore, a prostitute. God told Hosea to marry her (Hosea 1:2). Yes, God told a prophet to marry a prostitute!

I believe Hosea had grace to endure what he went through when his wife would sneak out at night, go sell and give her body to other men. They had a troubled marriage. And after an adulterous affair God instructs Hosea to take Gomer back (Hosea 3:1). God told Hosea to buy his wife back to redeem her and reestablish marital bonds. He paid money to get his wife back! This is a true story and testimony of our unfaithfulness to God and God's love for us. It is also an illustration of the ability we must forgive and love others because greater is He who is in us than he who is in the world.

Satan loves to lure spouses outside of their covenant. He is sneaky with it. He targets and attacks the weakest link. He uses addiction, lust, pornography, and lies. It is his intent that the spouse who had been betrayed by unfaithfulness will give up and walk away from the covenant. Then, he wins.

Listen, I am not trying to guilt you into staying in a marriage that has been plagued by adultery, or abuse for that matter. I get it. I have been married twice and the things I have endured were painful. Nowhere does it say that we are obligated to sit and take the pain, especially when it is repeated, or the unfaithful spouse is unrepentant. Ouch! However, we must forgive. Then, what we do with that forgiveness is between us and God.

I am not trying to tell you that God said to stay. That is not my place. Yes, God hates divorce. He also hates a lying tongue, haughty eyes, and other things.

I believe God hates abuse, too. He loves us too much to make that the intent or expectation.

At the same time, what a mighty God we serve who can take a broken marriage union where love seemed loss and all hope was gone and turn it all around! God masters in restoration. Restoration means to make new. He can make your marriage over as if nothing ever happened!

Will that be your story? I do not know, my dear. What I do know is if you trust God, if you stay in alignment with His word, do your part and **stand** on His word, He is faithful.

It is possible to love after adultery. It is possible to love after abuse. It is possible for a cheater to be delivered. It is possible for an abuser to be delivered. It is possible to heal after being cheated on and/or abused. With God all things are possible! That is what the scripture says. You must seek God for yourself and your marriage to determine what is the best choice for you. God is not a respecter of persons. If He can heal one marriage that endured adultery or abuse, He can heal another. The challenge is we do not know how long it will take and what will be required of us and many give up in the process. No judgement here. I get it. I gave up on my first husband and I almost gave up on my current husband.

Remember, an abuser has often been abused or they have witnessed this behavior and taken it on as normal and acceptable. If you are the abused, this is probably not your first go round. Healing is critical. Therapy is necessary. Separation may be in order so that both spouses can be delivered. If separation becomes the solution, remember to separate with Godly counsel and a clear plan and path to reconciliation.

When it comes to adultery, something I want you to under**stand** is it is often not personal. What does that mean? When a spouse cheats, it is often not to purposely hurt the other spouse. Cheating is a symptom of a deeper problem within the cheater. Typically, cheaters have experienced childhood trauma, such as sexual abuse. Most cheaters have been cheated on or have an unhealthy outlook and misunder**stand** the purpose and sanctity of sex. It is NEVER the person being cheated on who is the problem or blame for the cheating. You may have acted out or upset your husband, but that is not a reason to cheat. In fact, there is no reason to cheat.

Cheating is a choice, not a mistake. When a cheater blames their partner or spouse for their unfaithfulness, it is shift blaming and deflecting. A healthy person, a healed person, a person with integrity will not cheat. He or she will walk away from an unfulfilling relationship after trying to make it work. A cheating husband is a broken and wounded man before compromising the integrity of the union.

Keep in mind that if your husband has cheated or is cheating, it is not just on you. He has cheated or is cheating on God. He made a vow to you and God. He entered a covenant with you and God. The issue is much deeper than it seems, and it needs to be addressed. Just remember it's not personal in the sense of being an attack on you because it is not just you that is affected.

Prayer is a powerful antidote and necessary to overcome these and any type of challenge in marriage and in life. However, sometimes we need additional help and support. I encourage counseling, therapy, and coaching. My husband and I have utilized all the above and still do. The Bible advises to seek wise counsel and the best way to learn something you don't know is to learn from someone who does know. There is nothing wrong with getting the right help and support. Notice I said, *the right help.* Our family and friends may have sound advice for us but when it comes to your marriage it is best to seek counsel from professionals and those who do not have an emotional investment or tie to you and your husband.

Many marriages with issues, including abuse and adultery are a result of surface level compatibility and not waiting on God. It just means you jumped in before the work was finished and now the work must be done while in the covenant if you choose to stay in it. Ultimately, marriage will bring to surface all your unhealed issues, it will expose all your wounds, and all your unpacked baggage. Yet and still God can heal, deliver, and transform.

CHAPTER 6

Baggage Claim

When we travel by airplane, most of us take luggage or baggage. Some of us take one bag; some have a carry-on and a small personal bag, others take a suitcase that requires check-in. Then, there are those of us who tend to over pack. We are the ones who have too many bags and end up having to pay extra baggage fees for too many bags or because our luggage weighs too much. It is rare that a person travels by airplane without any baggage.

The same is true for relationships. It is rare and probably impossible to enter a relationship without *any* baggage. In this case, baggage is everything that you come with when you enter a relationship, specifically marriage.

When you entered marriage, you did so with your own beliefs, ideas, perspective, opinions, values, thoughts, and more. You had a set of

73

expectations, hopes, and ideas. You also had experience. You lived before meeting your husband and you went through things. All of this creates some sort of baggage or things you carry and when we enter marriage, we bring that stuff with us.

You may have shared some of your baggage with your husband before getting married. You told him things about yourself, your life, your interests, your upbringing, your hopes, your dreams, your friendships, and/or past relationships, etc. You may even think you shared everything, like I thought I did with my husband.

On our first date, we talked for 14 hours. I could have sworn we talked about everything! Yet, once we were married and in the thick of things, I realized how much we had not talked about. Can you relate?

Have you ever noticed when we travel there are times when we forget to bring items, or we do not utilize everything we packed for our trip? Sometimes we bring home clean clothes that were never worn or unused cosmetics. Other times we buy new clothes, cosmetics, and even souvenirs and we add these items to the baggage we are taking home.

When you got married there were some things that were still packed away. You had some baggage and so did your husband. Although you may have tried to get everything out of the bag, as I thought I had done, when you got married your husband and you both had some things that were still packed away. He may have opened his suitcase a little to share an item or two with you but sometimes we have so much packed that even we forget what's in the bag. It will not all come out until we get back home, or until time has passed.

For example, as we transition from childhood into adulthood, we carryover. Things happen as we are growing up that mold and shape us: How we are raised, what we see and define as a family, love, loyalty, etc. That experience or baggage gets carried into our relationships, and especially into marriage.

Depending on your earlier interaction with men, your baggage may be light, or it may be heavy. The same goes for your husband. He has experiences that have shaped his views and opinions about women in general, how to love them, how to treat them, how to be with them. He has brought that baggage (experience and perspective) with him into your marriage. That can be a good thing or a bad thing. Either way it is a thing that you will deal with.

When we are courting or dating, we don't pull our baggage out and unload. It takes time before we grant access to some things. Sometimes we do this on purpose; sometimes it is unknowingly. Those things that do not come up include every issue that we choose to not talk about while dating, the stuff that only comes out when something goes down. Things from our past, upbringing differences, and real reasons why relationships ended (because there are always two sides and we hear only one and that is what they tell us and present to us).

Marriage has a way of airing out your dirty laundry! Things you thought you dealt with or things you thought you were over sometimes come up in marriage. As we live with our husbands and experience life, things we may have forgotten about will be exposed and must be dealt with. When we don't deal with it, it will fester, grow, and become a problem. And it will stink.

THE ROTTEN EGG

When I was a little girl, my mother and I resided in an apartment where the hall closet was my toy haven. There was huge closet at the end of the hallway and all my toys were in it. On the weekends, I would pull all my toys out and there would be toys everywhere. When play time was over, I had to put all my toys back into the closet.

One day my mom identified an odor in the apartment. It was an awful odor! The place was clean, and she added bleach and Pine Sol to the bathroom and kitchen in hopes of killing the odor. Yet the stench remained, and it was strong for days!

She became fed up with not being able to find what was causing our home to smell so bad. She was determined to figure it out, however. I was assigned to take all my toys out of the closet and organize them, make sure they were clean and put away neatly. On my quest, I opened a container. It was a pretend pot that went with my other pretend dishes. Inside of the pot was one of my Easter eggs. Well Easter had passed days or weeks ago. The odor that released from the pot when I opened it caused me to drop it altogether. I had discovered the cause of the deadly odor in our apartment: a rotten boiled egg.

My mother could smell the egg long before I found it. I had to do some digging to discover the stench in the closet that had seeped in the entire apartment. Sometimes there are things in our past that stink. There are things we packed away or simply forgot about but over time that thing shows up with a stench that tries to kill everything in its path.

In marriage, you will be forced to clean out the old stuff and face some of the stinky things of your past. You will be forced to analyze some of the decisions you made or things that happened to you and how they really affected you and how they may be affecting your marriage. There is no way to live with another human being, sleep next to them, and do life with them without seeing every ugly side, every ugly part, and smell the stench of whatever was unpacked in their bag or closet. How you handle those things is what counts.

Of course, I had to throw away the rotten egg and the toy dish I had placed it in. Then, my toy closet had to be sanitized and cleaned because that stench affected everything it was near. It still took some time for the stink to leave the apartment even though the rotten egg had been thrown outside in the dumpster.

There are some things that even when you discover, expose, and address them the stink may linger. Give it time. Let it air out. Do what is necessary until the lingering smell has gone away.

In other words, some issues are going to take time before they clear all the way up. We do not get to determine how long it will take or how fast the stink will go away. You are not your husband's Pastor. You are not his mother. You are not his God. You are his wife. Be his wife. Be his partner, his lover, his support, his suitable helper.

He may do things that you do not approve of. He may do things that you disagree with. He will do things you do not under**stand**. Again, you are not his mother, his God, his Pastor, or his boss. You can express how you feel but do so with wisdom and tact. Sometimes you may have to take it to God and not even bring certain things up. You know your husband and you know the temperature of the atmosphere in your marriage. If it's hot, don't add coal or grease. There is a time to speak and a time to be quiet, remember? The Bible says so. Be wise about timing and be selective with your choice of words and presentation.

Therefore, it is important to pray. God will speak to you, lead, and guide you. God will give you insight on things. He will even reveal if there are hidden things or baggage that needs to be unpacked.

It is not our job to dictate what should be done, when or how. We do not get to determine our husband's process, growth, and/or maturity. Remember earlier I talked about being on different levels. Sometimes and in some areas, you may see eye to eye, and sometimes and in some areas you will not. It does not make you right and him wrong or vice versa.

Your husband is not called to be who you think he should be. He is called to be who God says he is, and you get to walk alongside him on the journey. You are called to be who God says you are. Focus on YOUR part, your role, your assignment, and your walk with God. Understand that change is inevitable. You both will change and that is normal. You have gotta ride out those changes and not become upset because he is not who you married.

When you said, "I do," you did not know everything you were committing to. It is impossible to know everything. Some things come out months, even years later. Some things develop over time. This is your marriage and your husband. Claim it. Just like we must claim our baggage at the airport when

79

the flight has landed, you must claim your baggage and the baggage your husband came with because you two are in the process and on the journey of becoming one.

I encourage you to do your best to remain committed to the commitment. Make sure you are doing everything you know to do. You can learn what you do not know, and it starts with the Word of God.

CHAPTER 7

Becoming One

Once Eve was presented to Adam as his suitable helper, the Bible says in Genesis 2:24, "and the two shall become one." Two people created with distinct differences, matched in holy matrimony, would now become one. How?

Become means begin to be or to come into existence. In marriage, becoming is instant and a process. It is instant because immediately after getting married two people are now viewed as one entity. For example, most government and court systems recognize joint ownership of all things within a marriage union. What's yours is now his and what's his is now yours. Hence the reason some couples consider prenups and others that end in divorce find themselves in court battling the split of owned and acquired items.

I believe in God's eyes that we become one when the marriage begins. The Bible says a sanctified wife sanctifies her husband (1 Corinthians 7:14). A sanctified husband also sanctifies his wife. *Sanctify* means set apart as or declare holy, consecrate, and purify or cleanse. If one declared holy and purified spouse can make the other holy and purified, to me that means He sees us as one. I know we are individuals and when we see God, we are accountable for ourselves, however when God sees you and I, as believers, He sees us through the lens of the blood of Jesus Christ. Hallelujah! He does not see our filth, mess, shame, and sin. We are joined to the Lord and have become one with Him (1 Corinthians 6:17).

It is for this reason that I believe when we pray, we must be careful. We should not go to God complaining about our husbands, cursing our husbands, yet expecting blessings in return. If we curse our husband, we are cursing ourselves. If we bless our husband, we are blessing ourselves. This is part of the instant state of becoming, in the spiritual.

There is a process of becoming in the natural. Two different people, in marriage, over time become more and more united. Think back to when you first accepted Jesus as Lord and Savior. You probably had some unholy ways about you and things that needed to change but it did not happen overnight. It took time and it was a process. Marriage is to mirror the relationship between Christ and the bride (the believer), so the same happens in the marital relationship. We enter marriage with baggage and with things about us that need to change. The change does not happen overnight in most cases. It takes time and it is a process.

We must under**stand** that becoming one with our husbands means there will be things we both need to work on and work at. There are some ways about us (and them) that need to change for the successful blending or merging or becoming. Both parties will have to adapt and adjust.

I remember sharing with a friend how my husband was not the same man I married. He had changed. As I was sharing things to make my point, God began to show me I was right. My husband was not the same man I married. Several years had passed and if he was the same that would mean there was no growth.

The goal is not to stay the same. The goal is to grow. The goal is to become a better version of yourself. The goal is to identify and walk in purpose. Right?

The man I married was my ideal of him. It was all that he presented and all that I saw and accepted. The real person did not come all the way forward until time had passed and that real person had real issues, needed real healing, to reach a real destiny.

You married who you thought your husband was. The person he really is may have taken some time to come forth. When we begin to see a different version of a person other than what was presented or who we thought they were, we start to think something is wrong. What if something is right? What if that was the whole point?

When I made the decision to marry my husband I did so based on limited information. The information I had is what he had presented. It was also what I had searched for or inquired about. It was also what his family and friends revealed to me. But that was all surface level knowing. There is a deeper knowing that can only exist once you enter covenant and the process of *becoming one* begins.

My husband and I met, became engaged, and married within seven months. This may not be your story. Perhaps you moved quicker or took much more time getting to know the man you married. No matter what there is only so much we can initially learn about another person and for many reasons.

If you do not live together prior to marriage you are going to learn a lot more once you start living together. If you do not sleep together before marriage you are going to learn a lot more once you start sleeping together. Even if you sleep together, live together and were close friends for years you will still learn things about one another that you did not know and sometimes it is because they did not even know or remember things about themselves.

Personally, looking back, I feel as if I didn't spend enough time with my husband prior to marriage. As much time as we spent together and even after that 14-hour first date of discussing what we thought was everything, there was still much more to learn. We were inseparable from the day we met, yet we still did not know one another.

My granny used to say do not marry a man until you have seen him angry. That is wisdom and I did not listen. The first time I saw my husband angry I was afraid and concerned. I had to learn what his anger looked like and how he operated while in it. That is another story and chapter.

Ultimately, the man you married was a representative of who your husband really is and now that the mask is off you are seeing a different person. Welcome to becoming one! As you see this different person it may feel and seem as if you married the wrong man. Well, you did. You married your ideal of him. But the man he was on your wedding day is not the same man he was the day after the wedding. He is not the same man one year, three years, or five years down the road, either. People change and we are supposed to. This is why the vows include "for better or worse." In addition to changing, we often have things from our past that resurface when we are not even expecting it to, or things come up that we may have forgotten about. Other times, reality just has not kicked in, yet.

In my case, my husband and I were not living real life initially. We had lived a fantasy during our summer courtship in Florida. My children were with their grandmother, his daughter was with her mother, and we were all over town living it up. We didn't have to discuss household chores, finances, paying bills together, sharing a bed, etc. The concierge and hotel staff cleaned my hotel room, took care of my dry cleaning, parked my car for me, and cooked breakfast for me, daily. My bills were on AUTOPAY, my job had fronted me money for meals, and tips, my credit was good, and I shopped and spent money like I was rich as I enjoyed my summer escape.

He would see his daughter on the weekend. Sometimes I would go with him and then we'd hit the town. His ex-wife did the dirty work of day-to-day care of their daughter. He lived as a bachelor, with a roommate, paying child support, dating a California chick, and free to do as he pleased. We were living it up and having a ball. Yet we did not know what real life together looked like. I did not yet know the impact of child support coming out of his checks. I was unaware of his day-to-day habits and he was unaware of mine. Although we were engaged, we were dating and we all typically put our best foot forward when we are dating. Afterall, that is not the time to drag out your suitcase into the room and unload. Oh no. We keep those things tucked away for as long as possible, sometimes on purpose, other times it is unknowingly.

I didn't know about everything that my husband was carrying, good and bad. He did not know everything I was carrying, either. No matter how transparent we thought we were, we were both unable to reveal things that we would only learn once we were living together, daily.

There are layers to your husband and layers to you. Just like he didn't know EVERYTHING about you when you married, you didn't know everything about him. Marriage is about growth and commitment. As you learn about the person you committed to you will grow more if you rock with them through the challenges than if you jump ship on to the next person who will also have baggage. They may have less baggage or a different type of baggage, but they still have baggage and the person you leave is abandoned because you chose to not keep your vow.

Speaking of vow...consider the vow you made to your husband and to God when you were married. Ecclesiastes 5:4 says, when you make a vow to God, do not delay in fulfilling it. You made a vow to your husband before God or in God's presence. The commitment is to the vow is to your husband and God. Most of us did not count the cost before we entered marriage. Most of us were sold on *better, richer, health,* and *forever.* We did not contemplate *worse, poorer, sickness,* and *until death do us part.*

Be honest, did you consider what *worse* might look like? Think of the worst thing that has happened in your marriage to date. Did you think that it would happen on the day you vowed "for better or worse?"

How about *poorer*? Often, we consider things like job loss, but job loss could lead to depression or even homelessness. What happens if the job loss is extended for months, or years? What about if the hard worker you married becomes lazy and doesn't want to work anymore? Based on the vows, that is not a reason to divorce or leave the marriage. Do you get what I mean?

Let's talk about *sickness* – we tend to think basic stuff like colds or maybe we consider things like a terminal illness diagnosis. But did you consider mental health? Did you do a mental check on your spouse before you said, "I do?" Did you ask if depression ran in the family or bipolar disorder or any other disorder or mental illness?

My husband was diagnosed with PTSD (Post Traumatic Stress Disorder) AFTER we were married. I had heard of PTSD, but I never heard of it from or about him. He did not know he had PTSD until I advised him to go see a Doctor based on some symptoms he was having. Of all the things we talked about in the beginning we did not talk about mental health or mental illness. *Sickness* includes mental illness, you know.

I knew that my husband had been in the military and there were some great disappointments, but the real impact was revealed after we took vows. His condition affected both of us. It has been a lot for me to bear. Early on, unknowingly, his condition triggered my own bout of depression, which eventually led to clinical depression, antidepressant pills, suicidal ideation, and suicide attempt. I have had to go to therapy to manage anxiety that developed from all the above. Have you considered this side of "in sickness and in health?"

How about pornography? That is a sickness. Pornography is sexual exploitation. Sex is sacred and to be shared only between husband and wife. It is a gift to husband and wife from God. We are not supposed to be watching other people engage in sex, especially people who are unmarried and performing for entertainment and/or money. Satan took God's design of sex and exploited it. As a believer in God and follower of Christ we should not be engaging in or accepting of our husbands watching porn.

Listen, I get that every case is different. The Bible is still God's Word and it's a holy Word. When we make a vow, we are expected to keep it. I am aware that some hurtful things happen in some marriages. Adultery is one of them. Abuse is another. Then, there is mental illness, financial irresponsibility, debt, blended family issues, in-laws, addiction, associations, unhealthy friendships, secret sin, and more.

What has been the *worse* in your marriage? Do you think God is surprised by any of it?

The man you married is not your husband. Your husband has changed, and he will continue to change. The woman your husband married is not his wife because you have changed and will continue to change. You are both not the same people you were when you met, and when you married, and that is okay. We must learn to navigate life and growth together. We must learn to extend grace, allow room for development, maturity, and experience. This is what is meant by *becoming one.*

Many of us see the first sign of trouble, worse, sickness, poorer, etc., and we are ready to run! I am guilty. I cannot tell you how many times I have said, "I did not sign up for this!" Or "Oh hell no, you've got me messed up! I am NOT the one!"

Truthfully, you really do not know what you signed up for because you are not God and you did not know what was ahead when you agreed to marry your husband. You had an expectation but where did that expectation come from? Also, just because you expected things to go one way does not mean that is how they were going to go.

What if your husband is your assignment and purpose? Many of us think our purpose or assignment is only connected to a job or career or business or ministry but those are temporary avenues and access points to do kingdom work which is why we are even on earth! We are here to build the kingdom of God. Nothing else matters. Yes, we have important assignments in the field or in the world, however if God has gifted you with marriage and his design for family, then that too is a part of your purpose. Of course, God can work His plan in your husband's life without you but is that what you want?

I remember I got so tired of dealing with things in my marriage that I told God I didn't want to do it anymore. I told him to assign someone else for the walk or the assignment because it was too hard. I didn't sign up for all that my husband and I have been through. Had God shown me any of it I would have swiped left and went on about my business. Nothing could have prepared me for the hurt I have experienced and endured in my marriages collec- tively. Both marriages put together cost me a lot and both marriages also taught me a lot.

God's power, God's healing, God's love sur- passes anything I could have faced as a married woman and in life overall. There are things my hus- band said to me that I did not think I could forgive him for. I remember saying, "We cannot come back from this!" But we did! There were deal breakers I put on the table and all of them were broken but I stayed. No, I did not betray myself by staying. I vio- lated boundaries that I had set without ever consult- ing God.

Boundaries are important. We need them in every relationship. They serve as a guide to let us know when someone has gone too far. However, we cannot set limitations on God with his own institution. Let me clarify that – you can do what you want, but if you want what God wants then what you want has to be forfeited. You must lay down your will to accept God's will.

What is God's will for your marriage? What is the vision for your marriage? The Word says without vision the people perish. Figure out the vision and the overall purpose for your union so that when all hell breaks loose, you have something to hold onto to and **stand** on.

In my case, God showed me His hand. He was present in it all. There were moments when I asked God what to do and I heard, "*forgive.*" There are moments when I did not ask what to do and I heard, "*forgive.*" Forgive does not mean accept mistreatment or misbehavior. Forgiveness may not always mean to stay where you are. I can tell you though that I learned what true forgiveness looks like right here in this marriage.

See, sometimes we talk a good game. We say we forgive; we say we have faith, but the proof is in the pudding. You don't know forgiveness until you have to love the unlovely, until you have to overlook and let go what hurt you. You don't know unconditional love until conditions come and you can remain in love. You don't know faith until you have to believe when nothing looks like what you are believing for.

So, my question to you is do you REALLY trust God? Do you really believe God? HE created your husband. He knows him better than anyone else. You being his wife grants you VIP access. In God's sight, you are the closest person alive to your husband. It doesn't matter if his mother or sister or best friend thinks they are the closest to him. Before God, YOU are the closest person to your husband, and you have access that no one else does.

Becoming is a process and it is instant and ongoing. As you and your husband grow and change, you will have to continue adjusting, adapting, and *becoming* one. You have everything you need to be successful at this. Read the Word, take God at His Word and **stand** on the Word, through it all.

CHAPTER 8

Without a Word

The Bible says in 1 Peter 3:1, "Wives, in the same way submit yourselves to your own husbands so that, if any of them do not believe the word, they may be won over <u>without</u> words by the behavior of their wives." The foundation behind becoming and being a silent warrior is this scripture. Sometimes we try to explain things to our husbands, and they don't get it, they don't under**stand**, or they do not value or respect what we have to say. This seems unfair and unjust.

I am a communicator. In fact, one of my degrees is in Communication. I like to talk, and I like to think I am fairly good at it. In business, I can give a presentation, teach a class, ace an interview, interview others, meet with clients, coach others and be effective. Yet in my marriage it seems like it is the one place I am not heard or able to communicate effectively. It is not because I do not try. When I began to pray about this, I heard God say I can make him (my husband) hear more, by saying less. That was hard for me to digest.

I felt like I needed to explain my points, express my feelings. Communication is key in marriage, right? Yet, if you are communicating and the other person is not understanding what you are saying then you are not effectively communicating. Effective communication is when you can deliver the intended message and the other party understands it. This is what makes it *effective*.

When you are constantly attempting to deliver a message and the other party is not receiving it, then what? In our case, as believers and as wives we have to take it to God. Pray. In fact, before you reach the place of constantly attempting – pause and pray. Before you even take something to your husband, before you express your thoughts and feelings, try to get in the routine of praying first. Allow God to season your words with what is necessary. Your words may need more love, more gentleness, more kindness. Take it to God before you to take it to your husband.

There are other times when we communicate something and the recipient, our husband, is not ready to receive it or just doesn't understand it. But if we pray beforehand this invites God in to reveal this to us. He may instruct you to wait or to say it differently or to not say it all. Pause and pray before you speak.

One of my prayer partner's, Sharon, says, "Weigh what you say." In other words, weigh your words before you deliver them. They could be too heavy for your husband right now. Weigh it out and wait it out. Remember it is by our ways not our words that we can win them over. Analyze your ways. Are you displaying the love of God before your husband? Are you operating in self-control? Are you being kind? Are you showing respect? Are you pursuing peace (with all men, especially your own man)? Are you being the woman God wants you to be in front of your husband in order to encourage him in his own faith walk? Start there. Let's take the focus off the man and put it on God and work on ourselves. Are you with me?

The role of wife is POWERFUL. The Bible says that a man finds favor when he finds a wife (Proverbs 18:22). Another friend of mine, Stacey, put it this way – she says, "You are your husband's favor factor." Good God Almighty! It is because of *you*, his wife, that he has favor. You are a blessing in your husband's life! Think about the man who doesn't have a wife. I mean, I imagine there is a blessing for him, but the Word specifies favor for the man who finds a wife.

A wife is gift and a treasure. She is assigned to help her husband. When God created Eve, it was because he identified that Adam needed help. He needed a partner. Adam could not fulfill his sexual needs. Many men, including Christian men, seem to think that porn and masturbation are the answer, to fulfill their sexual needs, and they think both are not sinful. I beg to differ. If I may interject briefly, as this may help you as well, masturbation is self sex. The fact that it is self-pleasure adds a selfish connotation to it, no? Sex is one of the benefits and pleasures of marriage. If you have a partner to have sex with, why would you need to engage in *self* sex? Is self sex a holy act that we can feel comfortable performing in the presence of God? Married sex is a holy act and guess what? You can invite the Holy Spirit into your bedroom, and you should. That is another book. Let me refocus...

God saw that Adam was alone and it was a problem. Adam could not navigate life or fulfill his purpose alone. God said Himself that it was not good for man to be alone (Genesis 2:18), so he created a suitable helper for him.

Why is it that we complain about things like helping our husbands find his keys, helping him fill out paperwork, preparing his lunch, scheduling a medical appointment, or doing certain things for our husbands when our role is that of a helper? On the flip side, why is it that we make suggestions, give advice, or attempt to help and our husbands reject us?

Can you see how the enemy can take this and use it to cause trouble?

We have to refocus our efforts and our energy. We have to focus on the assignment connected to the role and get out of our feelings. Feelings are fickle. They are unreliable and inconstant. We cannot rely on them. We can, however, rely on the Word of God. The Word of God says a sanctified wife sanctifies her husband. The Word of God says he may be won over without a word. Sanctify yourself and operate in a meek and quiet spirit, which is pleasing to God (1 Peter 3:4).

I know your husband needs prayer; mine does too. I know you are eager for some things to change; I am too. If there is nothing else, I would like for you to gain from what I share in this book or from my life, it is that we need to seek first the kingdom of God and its righteousness (Matthew 6:33). We have to get back to basics. We were made by God and for God (Colossians 1:16). Woman was made for man (1 Corinthians 11:9). Woman is not independent of man, nor is man independent of woman (1 Corinthians 11:11).

We were created to be here on earth to help build the kingdom of God. That is our primary purpose. You and I have gifts, talents, and abilities. We are many members but one body (1 Corinthians 12:12). Each member has a part to do for the body to be most effective. Let's focus on our part. Let's focus on being the best at whatever we have stewardship over.

Before you were a wife, you had purpose and power. Now, as a wife you have additional purpose and power. God desires that we seek Him and strive to do what He sent us here to do. Your marriage is a ministry. Yes, you are in ministry if you are married and if you have children that is another ministry. We have work to do and we are equipped to do it. If we make this our focus, and if we do all things as unto the Lord, we will begin to experience God on a deeper level.

If you feel like you married the wrong man, turn your face, your heart, and your focus to God. Start being the right wife, according to the Word, and see what happens. I am not telling you to be a doormat. I am not telling you to stay in an unsafe or abusive situation. What I am telling you is to first and always look to God and look in the mirror. You are not perfect. You have flaws. You make mistakes. You have baggage. Just like your husband. He may not be all that you hoped, dreamed, and thought but you probably are not all that he hoped, dreamed, and thought either. It's life. You can rid yourself of this man and get one who appears to be better than the one you get rid of and he may be. He may have a few better qualities, but I promise you he's going to do things to irritate, annoy, and upset you, too. You know why? Because we are human.

When you live with a person every day you see it all. You see the good bad and the ugly. You experience their bad days. You see and experience the unresolved issues from their childhood (baggage). You see their areas of immaturity. You see their brokenness, ignorance, and/or cockiness. You see who they say they are and who they present themselves to be. You see it ALL. Be ready for it. It is not about what you go through but HOW you go through it.

Going back to the book of Hosea, the prophet who was told by God to marry the prostitute. I read an article that described this union in comparison to our relationship with God. It said God is in a painful marriage with His people. It emphasized that the book of Hosea is a story that depicts God's knowing an understanding of those dealing with a difficult marriage. In other words, it is showing us what it is like for God to pursue our hearts when we run from him. Gomer ran from her husband to other men. We run from God to other men or things. We assume marriage is about our happiness but nowhere does the Bible speak of happiness in marriage. Marriage is about holiness.

The Word says that a sanctified wife sanctifies her husband (1 Corinthians 7:14). Our husbands are made holy by our holiness. That is something to hold onto and **stand** on because no matter where your husband is in the faith or if he has no faith at all right now, because of you he is made holy, he is purified and set apart. The enemy is limited to what he can do or even cause your husband to do. I know it may not seem that way at times, but this is what the Word says.

Let's reflect on the book of Job and how satan needed access to him. In fact, God offered Job, which means God knew Job would overcome. He also knew that Job would suffer, hurt, and ultimately become stronger as a result of what would happen to him and God was right. Job lost everything. His wife and friends cursed him, and he probably could not understand what was happening or why. Other people thought he must have not been serving God or living right based on what he was going through. Has this ever happened to? Has anyone every accused you of not living right because of all the hell you were going through? Have you heard the saying that God gives his toughest battles to his strongest soldiers?

What satan means for evil God turns it around for our good (Genesis 50:20). Your praying, believing, and standing will not be in vain. God sees it and He has all power in His hands to transform your marriage. If I can offer a higher level of hope, even if your husband never changes the way you are hoping and believing, God can change you to deal with it or move your husband out the way. The point is you have to know that nothing is pointless or useless. It is all for the glory of God and you will come out stronger if you allow the fire you go through to purify you, refine you, and make you better.

Some of us wouldn't know how to pray had we not encountered the painful things in our marriage. Some of us would have never fasted. It was when all hell broke loose that we became so hungry for God or hungrier for God. We started seeking His face, reading the Word, praying, confessing scripture, and sitting to be taught to learn *'what must I do!'*

The book of James 1: 2-4 tells us to "consider it pure joy when we face trials of many kinds because you know that the testing of your faith produces perseverance. Let perseverance finish its work so that you may be mature and complete and not lacking anything." Hello! There is it. You were made for what you have endured. You were made to overcome. We are more than conquerors; all we have to do is work the Word because the Word works!

I do not mean to be redundant, but some points are worth repeating. Jesus suffered. He took ridicule, shame, and a beat down. What makes you think you will not have to go through things in this life? Yes, it hurts. Yes, it seems unfair. Yes, you want the pain and torture to end but remember Jesus. He did not speak a word. He went through quietly, and He came out King of Kings and Lord of Lords!

Take up your cross, daughter of the Most High God. Hold your head up! Your sanctification covers your household and your husband. Remember, you are his favor factor. There are somethings your husband would not have if you were not in his life. There are some things he would not be able to do. Your role and position is just that powerful. He may not know or understand any of this. He may not even deserve the good woman that you are. But did we deserve Jesus dying for us and all the mess we have been in and done? Stop focusing on your husband and focus on yourself and your walk with God. Make your election and calling sure (2 Peter 1:10)! Make sure you are in alignment with God.

You cannot lose anything by praying. You cannot lose anything by fasting and standing on God's Word. You will become sharper, stronger, and fortified in your faith, if nothing else, and that alone is powerful. You were designed for kingdom work and how can you do the work effectively if you never go through anything??!

Our tests and trials make us stronger. You need solid spiritual muscles to fulfill your purpose. The tests and trials that are allowed to come your way are to equip you, to exercise your spiritual muscles so that when you need to apply the strength you gained, you are ready.

There is a war going on. Your husband's soul is at stake. This is a serious calling and quite honorable! You have what it takes to conquer and to win!!

CHAPTER 9

Flight or Fight

You must make a decision. No matter what your marriage has encountered you have to choose to stay or go. In other words, you need to determine if you are going to stay and pray it through or walk away with a divorce decree. Either way there is gonna be some pain and hard work.

Flight
Divorce was never God's plan for marriage. The Bible says that God hates divorce (Malachi 2:16). Hold on...don't close the book and walk away because divorce is something you have contemplated or strongly considered. I am not here to judge you. I have been divorced and my current marriage pushed me to the point of considering it, again.

Divorce is not a ticket to hell and God will not disown you if you *choose* to go that route. Notice I emphasized *choose*. Divorce is a choice. It is not always an easy choice or the best choice or the only choice. No one can make the decision to divorce other than you and/or your husband.

I believe God hates divorce because divorce hurts. It hurts the two who are married. If children are involved, it hurts the children, even when we do not see it. It hurts families and friends who are connected to the union and may have liked seeing the couple together or were really rooting for the union. It hurts finances. It hurts our faith. It hurts the intended illustration of the relationship between Jesus and His bride. Divorce hurts and it sucks.

In the book of Matthew 19, Jesus says Moses permitted divorce, but Jesus also reminds us that in the beginning this was not so, meaning divorce was not God's plan for marriage. Divorce was permitted under the law of Moses, due to the hardness of hearts of the people. The people gave up. They turned cold towards their spouse. They also did not have the Holy Spirit like you, and I have, to help guide through some of the difficult seasons within marriage.

Divorce was permitted because folks were tired for one reason or another and like so many today, they probably felt like if the marriage wasn't making them happy why stay. Are you more concerned with your personal and earthly happiness than truly fulfilling the law and walking out the

Word? No judgment or condemnation. I want you to really think about it. I want you to consider everything before making a decision.

Have you done ALL you can in your marriage? Have you prayed AND fasted? I don't mean just not eating for a few hours or the entire day. Have you fasted and sanctified yourself before God? Have you applied the Word as best you can, in all areas, focusing on God's truth? Have you sought wise counsel concerning your marriage? Have you and your husband tried accountability partners, a counselor, and/or therapy? Have you exhausted all human effort and all spiritual pathways to seeing your marriage work?

Well, the Word of God says, having done all else, **STAND**. And that is the overall message of this book. God's Word does not change. God's Word cannot return to Him void. God's Word shall accomplish the purpose for what it was sent forth. See, sometimes we declare something for one purpose and God has another purpose.

When I decided to divorce my first husband, it seemed like the right thing to do. I was much younger than I am now, and my faith was not what it is now. My ex-husband had issues I did not know how to pray for, on, or about. There was also adultery involved.

Filing the paperwork with the court felt liberating initially. I was a strong woman, and I was not putting up with this or that. I took the cheating personally. I took his issues personally. I had purposed in my mind and my heart that I was going to just move on, and life would be better.

It was a long journey. There were nights I cried myself to sleep during the separation as I prayed that he would just knock on the door. If he had knocked, I would have let him in. I wanted him to see his own faults, own them, and we move on. I was not going to say any of this, he just needed to do it, to prove to me that he wanted the marriage.

He never did. The divorced was finalized and life went on. I survived the next few years to come. I literally woke up, threw on jeans, a t-shirt, a hoody, tennis shoes, and a wig and went to work. I was a zombie. I was disconnected and a functional depressed person. I did not cook; I fed my children fast food. This was my life until I snapped out of it. I'd have to think about how long that took but it took long enough.

Something on the inside dies when divorce happens. We become one when we get married. When we divorce there is a tearing that occurs. Something has to tear for one to become two again. When something is torn there are fragments of it that splatter and those fragments are irreplaceable. Take for example a piece of paper. If you rip it in half, the point of the tear is where the fragments are. You can tape that piece of paper back together but parts of it are now missing indefinitely.

An alternative to divorce may be separation. In 1 Corinthians 7:10 the Word says, "To the married I give this command (not I but the Lord): A wife must not separate from her husband. But if she does, she must remain unmarried or else be reconciled to her husband." This scripture is clear about separation being temporary and the goal being to reconcile.

Separation must be carefully decided and with Godly counsel. The purpose should be clearly defined and agreed upon by both you and your husband. Separation does not mean let's date other people or sleep with other people. You really should not entertain others during a separation. That is not the point of it. You are still married when you are separated, even if you are legally separated you are still spiritually married before a Holy God who honors covenant. Both parties are supposed to be working on themselves, especially spiritually, during a separation.

This is not my opinion, this is fact. Even if one partner violates the covenant by committing adultery, you are still married. Some venture to believe, once adultery is committed the marriage is over. Please direct me to the scripture that supports this. Yes, the covenant has been violated and broken, however it is still a covenant. The Bible tells us to obey the laws of the land and if we refuse to do so we are disobeying God (Romans 13: 1-20). The laws of the land says that once you are married, you are not single until a divorce decree has been issued by the court. Separated or not, sleeping with a new body or not, married is married until it's not anymore.

Marriage was intended to be lifelong. The relationship between Christ and the believer is lifelong and marriage is supposed to mirror that relationship. The world has downplayed marriage. That was satan's goal. The world supports divorce. The courts do not care if you stay together or not. Their operation is not based on biblical principle. If you and I are going to be for real about our Father's business, then we must do what His word says. Our lives should not look like the lives of nonbelievers. We should not be divorcing as much as nonbelievers. We are the salt of the earth and the light of the world, we are supposed to **stand** out, our marriages are supposed to **stand** out.

We have the power to overcome anything we may face in marriage. Will it be easy? Probably not. How long will it take? Only God knows. When is enough, enough? Does Jesus have a limit on us and how much of our sin He covers? Does God have a limit on how many times we can repent and come back to Him? No pressure. No judgment. I am just saying....

We are human and some of us do not feel graced to continue dealing with what we have endured. Some of us married for ill intent and all the wrong reasons and although God can transform ANY marriage, the time it takes for some may seem too much. I get it. Only you can decide, precious daughter of God.

I personally support separation when abuse is involved. There may be other reasons that Godly counsel may advise a separation. In the case of abuse, as mentioned earlier in the book, both individuals should be seeking help. They should be receiving spiritual instruction, guidance, and professional therapy and/or counseling. It is possible to recover from abuse in marriage, but it takes a lot of work, dedication, and sacrifice.

Separating for any other reason could be dangerous. The enemy's goal is to isolate you from your spouse so he can do his work. Look at the Garden of Eden. Eve was alone when the serpent came and deceived her. This does not mean it is only the wife who could be deceived. Satan is coming for the head to destroy the entire family!

He's gonna put his best forward to try to lure your husband into things he has no business in, including another woman. When you two are not sleeping in the same bed, this attack is easier, especially if your husband is not strong in faith. The point I am trying to make is separation is like leaving your back door cracked when you lay down to go to bed. You may be safe all night or an intruder may creep in and attempt to rob your household.

If separation seems to be an option in effort to avoid divorce and get some help to strengthen your marriage, make sure there is a plan in place and make sure the separation is not long term. The Word says a wife is not to depart from her husband, then it says but if she does let her be reconciled. Reconciliation is the goal of any Christian marriage separation.

Although a tearing happens within those who divorce, God still heals and restores. There is life after divorce. There can be remarriage after divorce, too. The choice is yours...to take flight or to fight, to go or to stay.

Fight
I personally want to walk out the word and SEE God's salvation in my life while I am here on earth! I want to see what God promised. If anyone asks why I stayed in my marriage, these are my reasons.

I believe God. I believe God's word. I believe it now like I have never believed it before. I am certain that what His Word (the Bible) says is true.

By now we know good and well that in marriage there will be trouble. Period. In life, as a believer there will be tests, trials, and tribulation. You gotta go through and you gotta learn what is in this life for you to learn. You have a choice to learn with the one you've got, get another one, or learn on your own as a single woman. You must decide.

I am pro marriage. I am pro God's word. I have faith that we can speak to a mountain and it shall be removed. I believe God can restore any marriage and deliver all involved.

Deciding to fight for your marriage is bold and courageous. It is not easy either. You will go through. Some of us will go through more than others. Once you decide you have to **stand** on it and apply God's word. You cannot waver. This is not a game. It is a matter of life and death. Your marriage will live or die and that could all be based on your position.

As far as I under**stand**, God's will is always restoration, resurrection, and reconciliation. Just look at Jesus. He died and was resurrected. He walked the earth and was reconciled to His father through death. All seemed lost when he died but believers were restored in that we received the gift of the Holy Spirit that Jesus promised. Now, will restoration, resurrection, and reconciliation happen in every marriage? No. Satan works overtime to make sure the answer is no.

One spouse can gain a lot of ground and **stand** for healing in their marriage but ultimately it takes two. The other spouse must have a willing heart, even if the **stand**ing spouse has to pray for a while for that change to take place. The hard part is we don't know when or if that change will come in our lifetime. God is not going to force anything on anyone. Jesus **stand**s at the door knocking but He must be given access to come in. I mean, God can do anything but that is not how He does things. He wants a willing heart. He wants a genuine and authentic "YES, LORD."

Fighting for your marriage does not mean arguing and carrying on. The Word says that the weapons of our warfare are not carnal (2 Corinthians 10:4). Marriage is spiritually based. The attack on marriage is spiritual. You cannot combat a spiritual attack with carnal weapons.

To successfully fight for your marriage, you have to become and master being a silent warrior. You have to master prayer, walk in discernment, and be guided by wisdom. This is especially true if your husband is not walking in the faith.

When we pray with the authority that God has given us, things MUST changes. The Word says we are seated in heavenly places with Jesus and we have been given all power over the enemy (Ephesians 2:6 and Luke 10:19). If we have all power, then we can pray for transformation in our marriages and husbands. Will it be challenging and difficult? For some, YES! It depends on the baggage (and strongholds) your husband has. It depends on other things as well. Let us not forget Hosea and Gomer. How many nights did she dip out on him?

Fighting for your marriage is no easy task. It is going to require a lot of you. It may seem like too much for you, but I encourage you to put your total trust in God and His Word. I have witnessed God's transforming power in my marriage and other marriages. If He can do it for me and them, I know He can do it for you, again and again. We must be willing to do the work and put in the time. We also have to know that taking a **stand** alerts the kingdom of darkness and all hell may break loose. What do you say, sis? Are you taking flight? Or are you gonna stay and fight?

CHAPTER 10

Oh, Hell No

Once you decide to fight for your marriage, do not be surprised when all hell breaks loose. It is more likely than unlikely that it will, and we have to be armed and ready. Has it ever occurred to you that our military prepares for war daily? They train physically, they master their weaponry, they stay preparing for a war that is unplanned. There is no set date for war, however, they know it could happen at a moment's notice. They stay on guard; they stay ready. They do not know when it is gonna break out, but they make sure that when it does, they are prepared.

Did you know that there is someone literally guarding the borders of the United States of America, at all times? Oh, yes! There are soldiers serving as watchmen on land, in the air, and at sea protecting our country. They take shifts and someone is *always* watching. If a soldier falls asleep or is not in position to guard our borders and an intruder gets in, it could be fatal and disastrous for the entire country!

We have to operate the same way. We have to watch and pray. God does not sleep or slumber. He is keeping watch. He will reveal things to us and show us what to do and when. We have to be in position to hear from Him. We know the Bible says there will be trouble in marriage. It does not tell us when the trouble will come, where it will come from, or how it will come. We know it will come, however.

We cannot wait for the trouble to show up to get ready. We should be preparing daily. We should be praying daily. We should be fasting regularly.

Yes, fasting. The Bible says that some things will only happen if we fast and pray. Specifically, Jesus said in Matthew 17, "This kind cannot come out except by prayer and fasting." He was talking to His disciples after they attempted to heal a man's son. Notice I said *attempted*. They were unsuccessful. Jesus rebuked the demon that caused the illness in the son and it departed, and the son was healed. The disciples asked Jesus why they were unable to do what He did. He said it was because of their unbelief, they needed more faith, and they needed the power of prayer AND fasting.

There are some things in your marriage, in your life, and/or in your husband's life that are not gonna change with prayer alone. You are going to need to fast and pray. You are going to need to consecrate yourself before God and become serious about this walk.

Many of us are play Christian. We have a form of godliness but deny the power. We pray, here and there. We look the part, but we are not operating from a position of faith and authority. What do you think you were created for? If each member in the body of Christ does their part do you know how effective, we could be?

In the military, soldiers rely on one another. One wrong move by one soldier could cause the entire troop or platoon to suffer. We are soldiers in the army of the Lord. We have established assignments on this earth and God is counting on us to complete our assignment. We are not here for ourselves and our own happiness. We are here to conduct business, kingdom business! Will you do your part? Will you take a **stand** for your marriage, not for your own sake but for God's sake? Will you walk in the authority you have been given and walk in the power you have in order to overcome all the power of the enemy?

When we first under**stand** our purpose as women, then wives, it becomes easier to navigate not only life but also marriage. We were created with purpose. Remember, God made Eve (woman) after He identified that Adam was missing something. We (women) were needed. Creation was not complete until God made us. That is powerful!

You are necessary, woman of God. Your position means much more than you under**stand**. You are valuable. Even if your husband does not recognize your value right now that does not take away from it. You are anointed. You have everything you need to live a life of godliness and walk in your purpose (2 Peter 1:3).

You have to tell hell, NO! You have to take a **stand** against the enemy and be confident in God to do so. If you do not feel like you can do that, then there is a need for growth in your relationship with God. I challenge you to go deeper! I challenge you to get closer to God. Spend more time with Him. He is our General and we need to be able to hear commands and instructions from Him while we are here on this earth.

Do you under**stand** that as a believer there is nothing that enters your life without God's permission? Even if God did not send it, He has to allow it to come your way and if He allows it that means He knows the end result. God is not going to allow anything to happen to you to your demise. You have to believe, trust, and know Him and His Word. You have to obey His Word and follow His statutes.

His Word tells us we are more than conquerors and we are victorious. The battle is not ours; it is the Lord's. If we know that the end result is already victory, we have to learn to not become consumed with the process. What do I mean?

Why do we get all bent out of shape? Why do we get all upset and in our feelings? If God allowed you to face it, you are equipped to get through it and overcome it. His allowance means there is something we are going to get or gain or learn from what we face or encounter. That is powerful!

It reminds me of a video game. I have two sons so that is probably why video games came to mind. In some of these games they play, the main character sometimes has to take a route in the game to pick up tools or weapons it needs to defeat an enemy or win the game. Some of us need to go through some valleys to gather tools. Some of us need to climb some mountains for strength and until we learn to speak to the mountain and tell it to move. We have to pick up some tools and weapons that we are going to need when we reach the next level in life. If you don't pick up or gain what you are gonna need you will reach a point in your life where you are not prepared or equipped for what you face.

If you had to slay a giant wouldn't you rather have the slingshot in your pocket than to have to go looking for one, hoping you find one?! Nothing we experience is in vain. Even when we cause a mess on our own, it becomes a lesson that our Heavenly Father helps us gain.

Some of us are at a tired place right now. Some of us feel defeated right now. Oh, hell no! Do not allow the kingdom of darkness to wear you down and wear you out! Take up your cross sis, refuel and recharge. The reason you are tired and feel defeated is because you did not prepare for what came your way. So, when it came, it threw you for a loop. It threw you off guard. You fell asleep on the border. You fell asleep on your post. You were not prepared because you did not prepare.

Listen, we cannot afford to wait for the war to start to get ready. We must prepare, like our military. We must get ready in advance. We should be in training ahead of time. We should be in our armor and have our weapons ready, ahead of time. You know the saying, *"stay ready, so you don't have to get ready!"* Stay ready!

If you're mid-war, you have gotta stay the course until your victory manifests. Unplug to recharge. Go on a fast. Reset so your strength is renewed, and you are able to **stand**.

If you are not in war right now, stay on alert and be in tune to hear from our General, the one and only, true and living God. He will give you warnings, advice, and instruction. When He does, you must listen and obey.

I remember God telling me to pray against the spirit of adultery. It was clear as day. I thought it was related to a wife I had been coaching. Her marriage had already been attacked by adultery. So, I began praying for her and her husband. That is not what God said. He said, "Start praying against the spirit of adultery." I did not know then that He was warning me of what was planned by the enemy to attack my marriage.

In the military, soldiers are trained to take orders. You and I must be trained and disciplined to take orders from God. You can't stop praying. You can't stop reading the Bible. You can't stop declaring God's Word over yourself and your marriage. You can't stop praising and worshipping. You can't stop fasting. This is a lifestyle as believers. This is why we were created and what we were made for.

Satan does not stop plotting so why would we stop praying? The Bible says that our adversary, the devil, walks around as a roaring lion, seeking whom he may devour. He is looking for an entry way into your life, into your home, into your marriage. He is looking for you to turn your head away from being watchful, so he can slide in. Sometimes we are so foolish that we *give* him total access and invite him in.

I got so mad a few times that I told God and satan that satan could have my husband. I declared with my own mouth that if he wanted to do the devil's work then the devil could have him. Thank God for God! Thank God that He loves my husband more than me because what if I had the power to turn him over the way I did when I was in my feelings? My husband would be in hell right now. My God!

We have to be careful, sis. God did not authorize us to be influential and powerful beings to dismiss and disregard anyone, especially our life partners. We have to fight for their salvation, fight for their purpose and fight for the union we share. No, it is not always easy. You are talking to someone who was married to a convicted felon with an addiction. You are talking to someone who was physically attacked over suspicion, not proof, but suspicion of being a cheater. I have never cheated in a relationship, in my life! You are talking to someone who was pregnant, after multiple miscarriages, and found out her husband had been having an affair. Many days I wanted to give up and give in. I still struggle from time to time. Can I be real? All I know is to trust God because He comes through for me. He is my vindicator. He is my guide. He is my comfort. He is my strength. He is everything I need that I do not even know I need!

Purpose in your heart to tell hell NO! Hell cannot have your marriage or your husband or your children or your legacy or your purpose! Trust the process, sis. Get out of your feelings and focus on your assignment. Ask God what you are supposed to do concerning your marriage. If you are going to stay and fight for your marriage, you must be prepared and know how to **stand** no matter what comes your way.

CHAPTER 11

Spitting Fire

The power of life and death are in the tongue (Proverbs 18:21). Do you under**stand** what that means? You can speak life into your marriage or death. What you speak matters!

The power of your words is so great that it is not just about being quiet or shutting up. That is not the purpose of this book or the intent of the title of this book. I want you to under**stand** the power you have and that if you speak the right things, they will manifest. If you speak the wrong things, they will manifest!

Imagine planting seeds of destruction, seeds of doubt, seeds of negativity, and seeds of failure into a garden. What do you think will grow in that garden? Destruction. Doubt. Negativity. Failure. Now imagine planting seeds of hope, seeds of inspiration, seeds of positivity, and seeds of success. You will begin to harvest hope, inspiration, positivity, and success. What you plant (with your mouth); will grow (in your life).

The Bible says to call those things that are not as though they were (Romans 4:17). If what you do not like what is before you in your marriage, begin to speak what you want. More importantly, begin to declare God's Word and God's will over your marriage and your husband and watch what will happen.

Words have creative power. They can literally take shape and form. In the beginning, God spoke. He said, "let there be light," and there was light. Before He spoke it, nothing was there. You and I have that same power. Of course, what we desire and declare should be in alignment with God's will. In order to ensure it is God's will you have to know the Word.

I challenge you to begin to use your words to create the marriage you want. Do it before too much damage has been done or too much destruction. If that point has already passed, then just start where you are. Ask God to uproot every negative seed planted, fill the holes with the blood of Jesus, and give you fresh soil upon which to rebuild your marriage!

In my book, *You Talk Too Much,* I stressed the reasons why we need to be incredibly careful talking about intimate details of our marriage. We must guard what we speak about our husbands and our marriage because our words have so much power. Not just our words, but the words of others, too.

You may be upset with your husband, then run to tell your girlfriend every wrong and foul thing he did. Later, you have forgiven him, you two have moved on and now your girlfriend is telling her husband or another girlfriend what happened. While you and your husband have moved forward, the words are being replanted and fertilized because the person you told just spoke them, again. Sometimes we get to a place where we are over something but someone, we told is not over it so they continue speaking it and guess what – what they speak will manifest because words are powerful.

Yes, you can pray, and you can believe that those words are weapons and no weapon formed against you shall prosper. However, you created the weapon when you opened your mouth. You used your mouth to spit fire into your own garden. Now the good seeds are gonna burn up and be uprooted as the negative seeds take root and grow.

In the book of Jeremiah, chapter five, the house of Israel and the house of Judah had been utterly unfaithful to the Lord. They lied about the Lord. The Lord's reply in verse 14 was, "Because the people have spoken these words, I will make my words in your mouth a fire and these people the wood it consumes."

I am convinced that our words are like fire and we are to apply the fire to burn up what we do not want and anything that is against God's will. We are supposed to use our words to declare the Word, to build and to encourage. Yet, our words have the power to tear down and burn, too.

A wise woman builds her house and a foolish one tears it down with her own hands (Proverbs 14:1). I was a foolish woman every time I would go to a friend or family member and disclose personal things about my husband and our marriage. I planted seeds of negativity, doubt, insecurity, and more. When I should have been praying, I was talking...too much. We started off with a fresh garden and I killed every fruit in it until the garden was destroyed.

Have you killed the fruit in your marriage garden? Have you spit fire into your marriage and consumed the good things? I challenge you to make a shift. I challenge you to imagine your words are like fire and use them to destroy everything that is not in line with God's will for your marriage and your life. I challenge you to begin to take the Word of God and confess it over your marriage like never before. Begin to call those things that are not as though they were. Guard your own tongue and lips. Be careful not to speak another negative word about your husband or your marriage. I don't care how bad it is or how bad it gets. Think on and speak on the positive and cut off anyone who tries anything different.

When I say *cut off*, this could be literally or figuratively. Sometimes you have to stop another person from speaking negatively about your husband and your marriage dead in their tracks. Don't let another person bad mouth your man or your marriage! Even if what they are saying holds truth, dispel it and counter it with the Word.

You may have to stop talking to, associating with, or hanging with some folks who are sowing negative seeds into your marriage. I had a friend who blatantly told me she did not like my husband after we were married. It is one thing to not like something he may have done, but to blatantly tell me you do not like him is telling me you do not like me because we are one.

My husband had a single friend who liked to entice him to do things that single men do, like go to clubs, stay out late, and drink. Notice I said *had*. These are not the kinds of friends we need to entertain, be connected to, or engage with when we are in marriage covenant. Cut em off. Guard your marriage and guard your mouth.

The Bible is filled with scripture about the power of words. I am including a list of some of those scriptures in the back of the book (Verses) for you to read and come to know so that you under**stand** the power you possess. This book was never about making you shut up or encouraging you to shut up. It is about helping you to see and recognize the power you have so you can walk in it.

You and I have authority. We have been given all power over the power of the enemy. We can speak to a mountain (a problem, an issue, etc.) and tell it to move. So why are we climbing mountains or afraid when we see them? Speak to that thing and tell it to MOVE!!

As I shared earlier, we cannot wait for the attack to get ready. We must be ready, always. You must have a regular prayer life. You must read, abide by, and know the Word of God. You must incorporate fasting and make it a regular part of your lifestyle.

CONFESSION OF FAITH

Like my last book, I am including a confession of faith for you to declare over your marriage. A confession of faith is just what it says – a confession of what you believe to be true that may not yet exist in your life. The world calls it affirmations. We call it confessions because we are admitting, acknowledging, and revealing what we believe by faith already belongs to us and it is based on scripture.

I encourage you to read what I have included (in the back of the book) and at some point, create your own confession of faith based on scripture for your marriage. To create a confession of faith, here is what I recommend. Make a list of what you dislike in your marriage or problem areas in the marriage. Make a list of what may not be the best attributes of your husband. Make a note next to those items and categorize them as best you can. Search scripture related to each category or line item, then write the scripture with your names in it or write it in an affirmative manner so that you read it as a declaration.

Whether you read the confession of faith I have provided or create your own, or both, read them, over and over, until and after you see them manifest in your life. After a while, you will have memorized them and can recite them during your quiet time and throughout the day. Trust me, there is power in this process because once again you are speaking life and life and death are in the power of the tongue.

You can resurrect what has died in your marriage, with your mouth. You can have God's will for marriage and your life. Declare the Word. Spit fire – burn some things up and ignite some things so that the right seeds can be sown and grow.

FORTIFIED IN THE WORD

Please be guarded with your words and be careful not to speak what you do not want. After being afflicted by my husband and reaching a place where we could barely communicate, I began telling him to just find someone else, move on and leave me alone. I spoke "find someone else." Over and over and over. I spoke "leave me alone." Over and over and over. I said it to him, and I spoke it to my friends when I vented. Out of my mouth I said, "Girl I wish he'd just find someone else and let me go." I opened the door. I invited infidelity and adultery into my marriage.

God knows that is not what I wanted; however, principle is principle. Like the Word says, I was snared by the words of my mouth. I should have been praying when I felt like my husband wasn't listening to or understanding me. I prayed here and there, but I was not serious. I vented and I negated my own prayers. I also pity pat prayed when I did pray. I was not praying from a place of authority. I was not confessing the word faithfully. Do not be like me in this regard.

Now some may think "it don't take all of that," and for some it doesn't, and it won't. God knew what I would learn because of what I went through and what I learned is necessary for my purpose. After going through what I went through I can now share with you and others and I am sharing from a place of experience. You don't have to go through what I went through. Stop saying what you do not mean. As believers, we have a fruit of the spirit called self-control. Walk in it. Get your emotions in check. Get out of your feelings and focus on your assignment!!

We have to become fortified in the Word. Fortify means to make strong, to strengthen, and secure. We must position ourselves to be strong and secure in God's Word, **stand**ing on what God said, abiding in the truth, and holding fast to it until it manifests.

Be careful not to speak from emotion. Be careful to operate in self-control, be honest and real with your husband and God. We are married. We have to under**stand** that no part of this is about looking weak or simpin. If you are going to be vulnerable anywhere it should be with God and also your husband. Be careful to say what you mean and mean what you say, otherwise you will be snared by the words of your mouth! Position yourself to be steadfast, immovable, and take God at His Word concerning your marriage and your life! Fortify yourself!

DO NOT MOVE

I talked; I was quiet. I prayed; I cried. I let things go; I fought back. I tried to monitor his every move. I acted like I did not care about anything he did. I tried to tell God on him. I tried to leave. I filed divorce...three times. I tried it all.

The Bible tells us in Ephesians 6:11, to put on whole or full the armor of God so that we can take a **stand** against the devil's schemes. We are warned that our struggle is not with flesh and blood (Ephesians 6:12). It tells us that after we have done everything, to **stand**.

Stand means to have or maintain an upright position, or to be situated in a particular place or position. Our position must be trust God. No matter what we must trust God. The God who created you and your husband, the God who created heaven and earth, the God of Abraham, Isaac, and Jacob – we must trust Him. Sometimes life presents us with so many attacks that we run out of solutions in the natural. What if this happened on purpose? What if this happened to purposely get to you to trust God even in the midst of the impossible?

When you reach a point where you have done all you can God wants you to **stand**. He wants you to **stand** on His word. Be immovable. Be unbothered. Be steadfast. Counter very attack with the with the Word. That is your defense.

Do not attack your husband. Do not come at him foul, even if he is being foul. God is your vindicator! Go into your prayer closet and go before God. If you do not have a prayer closet, create one. Or go into the bathroom, the car, or get on your face in the bedroom or living room! Do what you gotta do. Build up your trust in God so much that you don't need to vent to anybody besides Him.

Talking about your problems or issues is not going to resolve them. You think it makes you feel better to get it off your chest, but truth be told most people cannot assist you with your problems anyway. They have their own problems to figure out. If you need someone outside of yourself, consider Godly counsel or maybe a therapist but do so with the agreement and/or support of your husband. If he doesn't want to participate at least make sure he is okay with you participating so you have the right kind of support. Make sure the counsel is Godly and biblical. Make sure the therapist or counselor shares the same foundational beliefs as you. Make sure goals are set so you are focusing and managing the time responsibly with counsel.

Do not move from the position of trusting God and **stand**ing on His Word. Seek Him in secret and He will reward you openly (Matthew 6:4). When it is all said and done your spiritual growth and walk with God will strengthen and grow and that is the point. God will get the glory from your life and that is the point.

The more I prayed, the more I heard from God. The more I heard from Him, the more I wanted to hear from Him. I needed to hear from Him.

Pray and fast. If you see no change or little change in your husband and marriage, pray more and fast more. You cannot pray and fast without reading the Word.

Be sure to guard your mouth concerning your husband and your marriage. Your response and how you handle things will be the determining factor to know if you have been praying for real or not. If you pop off, you still have work to do. If you cuss and slam doors, you still have work to do. Work the Word because the Word works!

CHAPTER 12

Love the Hell Out Your Husband

Love is more than a feeling. In fact, true love is not a feeling at all. For God so loved the world that He gave His only begotten Son (John 3:16). Love is action. God loved and God acted by giving up His Son.

There are different types of love and to have a lasting marriage you need the Ultimate love. God is love. We love Him because He first loved us. We know love and have the ability to love others because of God. God loves you and He loves your husband. He wants you to love one another.

It starts with love and it will end with love. Most people get married because they are "in love." Most marriages last because of love. Most marriages are restored because of love.

My husband and I hurt one another, and we did not know how to move beyond the hurting place. Sometimes when we are hurt, we hurt others. We tend to try to defend and guard ourselves. We may dish out what has been given to us, instead of countering it. The Bible tells us not to repay evil for evil. We are called to repay evil with good. How? The answer is love.

My husband and I were separated and had not talked in a few weeks. I had filed for divorce, again. God gave me an instruction for my marriage.

With tears welled up in my eyes, to the point I was unable to see, I said aloud, "I don't even know why I still love this man!"

Then, I heard, "You love him because I AM LOVE, and I AM in you."

I was upset with my husband and I felt like he did not deserve me. The power of God and the love of God swooped in, comforted me, and showed me things from a different perspective.

I began to see my husband as God sees him. I began to rise above the circumstances in order to focus on the purpose. I began to pray, like never before, and I began to fast for real. Please understand that in my own place of hurt I did not want my marriage anymore. It made no sense to stay. It made no sense to keep trying. There was period of time when I did not even want to pray for my husband. I felt like it was not worth it.

Then, one day, I heard God say, "When is a soul not worth fighting for?"

None of it made sense to me, yet it made faith and I had to be obedient.

There is a remedy in God's Word that will help you love as if you have never been hurt and it will help you love the hell out of your husband. A lot of wives say they have unconditional love for their husbands, but you really don't know that you have unconditional love until the conditions come and you can move past them. This is not to suggest that moving past anything is going to be easy. In fact, there will be very painful and difficult moments when you are trying to walk in forgiveness and love.

There are some things that are embedded in your husband. These are hard places. This is some of the baggage we discussed earlier. Just like Jesus loved us through the hard places, we have to learn to love our husbands through the hard places.

Your role as a wife is instrumental to your husband's purpose. Adam was incomplete without Eve. There are some things that need to develop in your husband, and it will happen through you.

You are allowed to be in your husband's life for a reason and a purpose. Trust that God has ultimate power to either transform the man and your marriage or to enable you to be set free from the marriage. I personally believe God can transform any marriage. Yes, ANY marriage! Your responsibility is to trust God.

My first marriage ended in divorce. But there was purpose connected to it. At the time, I did not have the faith to pray that husband through the issues he had. I took it all personal and walked away. In hindsight, I see where prayer could have helped. Many of us give up too soon. We get away from walking in love and adopt the mindset that we deserve better or God did not intend for us to go through what we may have experienced. I cannot speak for everyone and I am not here to judge anyone. The Bible says if we suffer, we shall also reign with him (2 Timothy 2:12). I mentioned this earlier, but do we really think we deserve a perfect life free from any suffering? We have sinned and fallen short. Some of us have some things in our past that we would never want others to find out about. Jesus was blameless. He did not sin at all. Yet, He suffered. Who do we think we are to think that we may not have to endure some difficult things, especially when the Word says so?!

Please under**stand** I am not trying to guilt trip you. More than anything I want you to under**stand** the power you have when you walk fully according to God's statutes, when you pray, when you fast, and when you trust God.

Focus on your walk with God. Make sure you are walking in love. When you keep your eyes on God no matter what is going on either things will turn around or you will be released but do not move until you have been released. When I say released, let me be clear. I personally do not believe that God tells any of His children to divorce. The Word says God hates divorce and God is not a man that He should lie. I do not believe He will tell anyone to do anything that He hates. I do believe that God knows the heart of our husbands and He knows if the man is going to surrender in this lifetime and whether or not your journey will be extremely challenging, difficult and or dangerous. God allows us to make our own choices and He will show us things and allow us to see things. Then, based on the information we have, the decision is up to us.

Release means allow or enable to escape from confinement. Getting married is a personal decision that we make and therefore we can decide to stay in it or get out of it. The purpose of marriage was intended to be lifelong, however. Divorce is a choice and there are times when it has proven to be a good choice, but I am firm on the fact that the Word works, if we work it!

You and I have authority over the demonic attacks we may face. The tests will come. The trials will come. But the testing of our faith worketh patience. Your faith must be tested and tried to be proven true. You can believe God for a job and a car, but can you believe Him for your husband's salvation? Can you believe Him for your husband's deliverance? Just because it doesn't come when you want and the way you want doesn't mean God isn't working. Are you even ready for your husband to be transformed? If God gave you a miracle right now and delivered your husband, cleaned him all the way up, brought him back home, whatever it is you are believing for, are you ready to **stand** with him and serve God? Is your life, right? Can you handle him becoming a minister of the faith right now? Can you lay hands on someone possessed or oppressed and pray that spirit off them?

We are in this world but not of it. The expectation and **stand**ard by which we are called to live is not like everyone else or like the world. The world says if someone wrongs us to seek revenge, retaliate or cut them off but God's Word says to forgive, turn the other cheek, offer them the coat off your back, and love them. The same applies in marriage, the most powerful institution on this earth and the foundation for family.

When a spouse sins against the other, we are called to forgive. We are called to love. You can love the hell out of your husband just like God loved the hell out of you. Do you HAVE to do it? No, you have free will but there is a blessing on the other side of obedience.

Remember, God told Hosea to marry Gomer. God knew she was a hooker and a cheater, but he told Hosea to marry her. When she went out and back to her ways God told him to go get her. He was her connection to salvation! What if you are your husband's only way in or only way out? What if _this_ is your calling?

Often, we think our calling is tied to jobs or careers, but I am compelled to believe it is tied to people. We are not here for jobs and careers. We (believers) are here to do the work of our Father. There is a war going on and you and I were called to be a part of the war and we are on the winning team. The battle is not ours; it is the Lord's, but we are warriors, and each have a role to play in the battle.

There is one body, but many members and each member should do its part for the whole body to function the way it was designed to. If you are the right arm of the body and you decide you are not going to do what an arm is supposed to do the body will suffer. Another part of the body has to overcompensate due to inactivity on your part. Same goes for kingdom work. If you decide to opt out every time something bad happens, you are not doing your part and others have to overcompensate.

Take a **stand** for the kingdom. Take a **stand** for God's Word and His truth. God will honor your efforts and what you do in secret (for Him), He will openly reward. Go to bat for your husband and your marriage. Take a **stand**!

God honors covenant and the Word says that He wishes that none should perish so it is my belief that God can heal and restore any marriage, even one plagued by adultery, infidelity, and/or abuse. You were not called to this position of wife to sit on your husband's arm and look pretty. Nor were you called so you can just cook, clean, and pop out babies. Marriage is ministry. You were called to help this man come into his rightful position and stay there to finish the kingdom work assigned to him in this life. He needs you praying for him and seeing what he cannot see. He needs your *help*!

Your marriage is not going to look like every other marriage. This is a personal journey. Focus on YOUR walk with God and staying in alignment and right **stand**ing before Him. I cannot guarantee that your marriage will last. I cannot guarantee that my own marriage will last, but what will last is God's love for us and His Word.

Make sure that whatever you do, you do it as unto the Lord. If you gain a lasting marriage by **stand**ing on the Word, GREAT, but even if all you gain is a stronger walk with God, and more awareness of yourself then isn't it all worth it?

As a reminder, the Word of God says that we have been given all power over the power of the enemy (Luke 10:9). This means when all hell breaks loose, we have power over it! Come hell or high water, you can be victorious in marriage! Walk in love and when it is all said and done, we have the victory through Christ Jesus! All we have to do is **STAND**! Love covers, love conquers, love never fails, and **LOVE WINS!**

Confessions of Faith

You Talk Too Much Confession of Faith

(The following confession is a compilation of the short prayers at the end of each chapter from the book *You Talk Too Much: A Wife's Guide to Becoming a Silent Warrior*)

I open my lips to speak what is right. My mouth speaks what is true. My lips detest wickedness. All the words of my mouth are just; none of them are crooked or perverse.

I am a peacemaker, and I am blessed. The words of my mouth and the mediation of my heart are acceptable in God's sight. I rejoice in hope, I am patient in tribulation, and I am constant in prayer.

I am a wife of noble character. My husband's heart safely trusts in me. I am a help to my husband and a blessing in his life. With me by his side, my husband is a mighty man of valor and everything his hands touch is blessed.

I pray for my husband, daily. I am attentive to the Holy Spirit and always know what to pray for concerning my husband. I am confident that God hears my prayers and because I am confident that He hears me, I know that He has answered me.

I respect my husband. I show proper respect to him when we are together and when we are apart. My conduct and behavior is pleasing to God and because of my obedience, I am blessed.

I love my husband. I desire my husband and my husband desires me. My bosom satisfies my husband all the days of his life. His heart is turned towards me and my heart is turned towards him.

I am intentional with my mouth and my words. I bless others when I speak. I encourage others when I speak. I give hope when I speak, and I speak in love. I walk in love towards my husband and within my marriage. I allow love to cover and conquer all.

I will confess the Word of God in faith and confidence. I will declare God's Word over my marriage, my husband, myself, my family, my finances, and my life. The love is renewed between my husband and me. My marriage is strong, solid, loving, and lasting.

A Marriage-Related Confession of Faith

I am a virtuous wife of noble character.
I am a confident woman of faith.
Christ is the head of every man.
Christ is the head of my husband.

My husband is my head, and my husband loves me as Christ loves the church. My marriage is held in high honor among all. My marriage bed is undefiled. My husband is anxious about pleasing me (1 Cor 7:33).

As the word of God says, I learn quietly with all submissiveness. I am meek and quiet, which is pleasing to God. I respect my husband.

I am a sanctified wife. I am set apart. I am holy,
My husband is holy, for the Word says that an unbelieving husband is made holy because of his wife.

My husband and I love each other earnestly. We submit to one another. We do no repay evil for evil, we do all things as unto God.

We do not deprive one another. We walk in love.
We are no longer two but one flesh. What God has joined together, let man not separate.

I am subject to my own husband. He is won over without a word and by my respectful and pure conduct.

My adorning is of the hidden person of the heart with the imperishable beauty of a gentle & quiet spirit, which in God's sight is very precious.

My husband controls his body in holiness and honor. My husband calls me blessed and he praises me. His heart safely trusts in me and he will have no lack of gain. I do him good and not harm all the days of my life. My bosom fills him at all times with delight. My husband is intoxicated always in my love.

I am self-controlled, pure, working at home, submissive to my husband that the Word may not be reviled (Titus 2:5)

My husband loves me and is not harsh with me (Col 3:19). My husband lives with me with under**standing**, showing honor to me as the weaker vessel and joint heir with him of the grace of life so his prayers are not hindered (1 Peter 3:7)

My husband loves himself and his body and he loves me as his own body. He who loves his wife loves himself. (Ep 5:28)

My husband provides for me (1 Timothy 5:8) and he enjoys life with me. I am his portion in life and his toil (Eccl 9:9) He has cleaved to me and holds fast to me.

Verses

For personal reflection in NIV translation.

The tongue has the power of life and death,
and those who love it will eat its fruit.
Proverbs 18:21

A good man brings good things out of the good stored up in
his heart, and an evil man brings evil things out of the evil
stored up in his heart. For the mouth speaks what the heart
is full of.
Luke 6:45

Do not let any unwholesome talk come out of your mouths,
but only what is helpful for building others up according to
their needs, that it may benefit those who listen.
Ephesians 4:29

Those who guard their lips preserve their lives,
but those who speak rashly will come to ruin.
Proverbs 13:3

Do not repay evil with evil or insult with insult. On the con-
trary, repay evil with blessing, because to this you were
called so that you may inherit a blessing.
1 Peter 3:9

The soothing tongue is a tree of life,
but a perverse tongue crushes the spirit.
Proverbs 15:4

Even fools are thought wise if they keep silent,
and discerning if they hold their tongues.
Proverbs 17:28

But I tell you that everyone will have to give account on the
day of judgment for every empty word they have spoken.
Matthew 12:36

My dear brothers and sisters, take note of this: Everyone
should be quick to listen, slow to speak and slow to become
angry.
James 1:19

Sin is not ended by multiplying words,
but the prudent hold their tongues.
Proverbs 10:19

A person finds joy in giving an apt reply—
and how good is a timely word!
Proverbs 15:23

A gentle answer turns away wrath,
but a harsh word stirs up anger.
Proverbs 15:1

A gossip betrays a confidence,
but a trustworthy person keeps a secret.
Proverbs 11:13

Words from the mouth of the wise are gracious,
but fools are consumed by their own lips.
Ecclesiastes 10:12

What you have said in the dark will be heard in the daylight, and what you have whispered in the ear in the inner rooms will be proclaimed from the roofs.
Luke 12:3

And when you pray, do not keep on babbling like pagans, for they think they will be heard because of their many words.
Matthew 6:7

Out of the same mouth come praise and cursing. My brothers and sisters, this should not be.
James 3:10

Be wise in the way you act toward outsiders; make the most of every opportunity. Let your conversation be always full of grace, seasoned with salt, so that you may know how to answer everyone.
Colossians 4:5-6

Gracious words are a honeycomb,
sweet to the soul and healing to the bones.
Proverbs 16:24

Fools find no pleasure in under**stand**ing
but delight in airing their own opinions.
Proverbs 18:2

Keep your tongue from evil
and your lips from telling lies.
Psalm 34:13

About the Author

Tanya Denise is a self-published, international best-selling author, anthologist, and writing coach. Born Latanya Hampton, in Pasadena, California, Tanya has been writing since she was a young girl, beginning her journey with poetry and short stories, then gradually growing into newsletters, newspapers, independent magazines, journals, and books. In her working career, Tanya developed a digital corporate newsletter and was appointed Editor-in-Chief for a large corporation. She later became a website & social media content manager. Tanya has successfully written scholarship applications and grants, securing funding for her education, and large nonprofit organizations.

Tanya is a former higher education Admissions Advisor. She is an advocate of higher education and is currently pursuing a Master of Arts degree in Marriage & Family Therapy. She holds a Bachelor of Science degree in Communications, with a concentration (minor) in Communication and Technology. She also holds an Associate of Arts degree in Liberal studies, and two technical education certificates, as a computerized Administrative Assistant and an Accounting Clerk.

In 2019, Tanya birthed the Ardena Marie Carter Memorial (AMCM) Scholarship fund, an education award for at-risk, female, high school seniors. The award was created to honor her friend from high school whose life was tragically taken by domestic violence. In 2020, she created a scholarship program for aspiring, female authors.

Tanya is a serial entrepreneur; a survivor of domestic violence and she is a certified Domestic Violence Specialist. She is most notably known for her anthology series *Pretty Sad* - which includes five volumes of stories about the extraordinary strength of women who have overcome trauma, including abuse, addiction, depression, prostitution, and more. In 2019, Tanya founded Love Wins Publishing (www.lovewinspub.com), to assist new and aspiring female writers in becoming published authors. She has published more than 42 of her own works and she has helped more than 125 women become first-time published authors. Tanya has a passion for helping others and giving back to the community. Her passion has led to the receipt of several community awards, including Woman of the Year by the Antelope Valley Ad Hoc Committee on Education.

As the founder of the #timetotell movement (www.timetotellmovement.com), Tanya's purpose is to utilize her proven faith in God to serve as a catalyst to help others heal and operate in their gift(s), through her writing and business ventures. Her mission is to use her gift of writing to help women and empower them to walk in their purpose.

With a passion for finance, Tanya is a licensed insurance agent, and she enjoys taking cruises, reading, and learning. She is a passionate writer, speaker, and coach. She is also a mother and a wife who resides in Southern California. For speaking engagements and/or more information, please visit www.tanyadenise.com or contact admin@lovewinspub.com

You Talk Too Much

What is it like being married to you?

Are you operating in your role as a suitable helper? Are you respecting your husband as the Bible advises? Are you praying for him? Are you helping him? Or are you hindering him?

Explore these questions and much more in *You Talk Too Much: A Wife's Guide to Becoming a Silent Warrior.*

Will you use your influence to build your marriage or to tear it down?

Available on Amazon.com

The Silent Warrior Challenge

Check out the companion to *You Talk Too Much* - ***The Silent Warrior Challenge: You Talk Too Much Journal Workbook***!

The 30-day Silent Warrior Challenge is introduced on You Talk Too Much. The journal workbook will help guide you through the challenge and into a developing a deeper, stronger prayer life. The journal workbook includes reflection questions and exercises to help you to connect or reconnect with your husband through an active prayer life. This tool will lead you on an exploratory journey that will help transform your marriage.

Available on Amazon.com

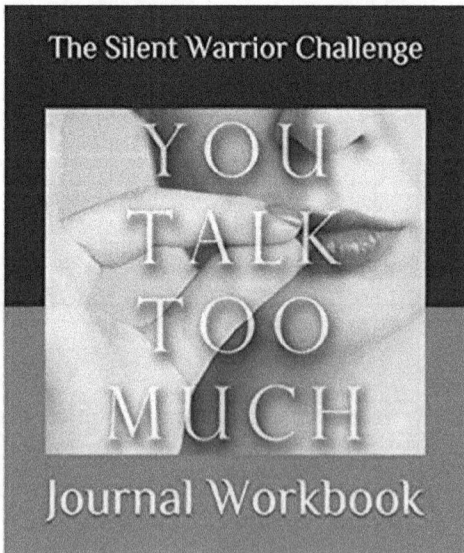

Acknowledgements

Dear God, thank you for not giving up on me when I wanted to give up on myself. Thank you, for courage, strength, direction, and clarity in all areas of my life, and especially in marriage. I want nothing more than to please you and do your will. Not my will but thy will be done, in the name of Jesus. Amen.

Dear Husband, it's been a journey and we are still on it and in it together. To God be the glory, forever and ever. Thank you, for supporting this book project and for your willingness to let God use me.

***

Since I started my journey in marriage the second time around and since releasing my first book on marriage in 2018, so many wise women have helped me become a wife of noble character. I purposely surrounded myself with Christian women who were seasoned in marriage so I could learn what I did not know.

I do not think I can remember them all to name them all. If we have ever had a conversation about life, love, marriage, and God, then you probably sowed into my life unknowingly and for that I thank you.

There are a few women who confronted demons with me, got IN the battle to help me fight and those I must call out.

We Mean Business – Audrea, Tam and Venus – I do not have the words to describe how grateful I am for my connection to you ladies. So, I will not even try. Just know that I love and appreciate you more than you know. Thanks for the group calls, group chats, group prayers and especially for the one-on-one chats and prayer.

Silent Warriors - Shamiya, Sharon, and Fotima – These are big guns with no hesitation to go head on with the enemy. Since our prayer and fasting, things shifted in my marriage and in my life. I felt like I was fighting alone, and I was wearing myself out. When I needed help, I called to God and he sent you three to join forces with me and we won! Thank you, thank you, thank you!!

Maya and Anjanette – Silent Warrior (married) group admin. Thank you for your commitment, time, dedication, and service. You two inspire me more than you know. I am grateful for our friendship and sisterhood.

Xandra Washington, Sherry Pitts, Camile Jene, and Keci Monique, thank you for the words of encouragement, your support, and your prayers.

I also want to shout out and acknowledge Pastor Sandra Webster Perez, Priscilla Hernandez (Mama P), and Linda Wallace (Mama Linda), for your wisdom, love, and grace.

Helene, Dr. Ivy Chandler, and Dr. Foglesong – my wellness team – thank you for your time and sacrifice to me and to others. Thank you, for helping me process and sort through the mess to make sense of what is best for me.

Lastly, to my mother-in-law, Dr. Olivia Jones Mack, for encouraging me to walk in my calling as a prayer warrior, more so a *silent warrior*. Prayer works.

www.ingramcontent.com/pod-product-compliance
Lightning Source LLC
Chambersburg PA
CBHW071444090426
42737CB00011B/1769